THE COMPLETE
HEINZ
COOKBOOK

THE COMPLETE
HEINZ
COOKBOOK

Colour Library Books

Contents

All recipes supplied by H J Heinz Company Limited
Photography by Peter Barry
Recipes styled by Helen Burdett and Siân Davies
Designed by Alison Jewell
Edited by Ros Cocks

CLB 3253
Reprinted in 1994
© 1993 Colour Library Books Ltd, Godalming, Surrey
All rights reserved
Colour separations by Advance Laser Graphic Arts (International) Ltd. Hong Kong
Printed and bound in Hong Kong
ISBN 1 85833 029 7

HEINZ – THE BEGINNINGS

Heinz varieties have become the grocery essentials of every family in the land. It all started in 1860 when an American boy of 16 began to bottle dried and grated horseradish from the family garden of his home in Sharpsburg, Pennsylvania. Unlike others, he packed his product in clear bottles, so that his customers could see he was selling only horseradish – without pieces of turnip or other cheap fillers. His name was Henry J Heinz and although he could not have known it then, he was starting a venture which was to grow into one of the world's great food enterprises.

By 1869, he had formed his company. Early struggles and setbacks were overcome and Heinz pickles and other bottled products began to appear locally. Henry J Heinz' claims – no artificial preservatives, no impurities, no colouring matter, plus a reckless money-back guarantee if his products failed to please – were unheard of in those days.

Quality and quality control have been the hallmarks of Heinz products ever since. The guiding principles of the founder have been handed down through the years; the most important simply states:-

To do a common thing uncommongly well brings success.

Henry J Heinz' elegant little business prospered and just over one hundred years ago, he decided to try his hand in Britain. Armed with samples of his products, he took a hansom cab to the renowned Fortnum & Mason in London's fashionable Piccadilly. The response of the store's chief grocery buyer was immediate: 'I think, Mr Heinz, we will take the lot'.

It was the start of a Heinz commitment to Britain which has led to a business now selling over 360 varieties every year, including soups, tomato ketchup, baby foods and, of course, their world famous baked beans.

Heinz Nutrition

Heinz have always made it their business to take nutrition seriously and are committed to producing good food from quality ingredients. The policy has always been to avoid using artificial colours and preservatives wherever possible. This dates back to company founder, Henry J Heinz, who was a leading figure in the US campaign for Pure Food Laws.

Today, practically every home in the UK uses at least one Heinz product every week of the year. The concern for quality and purity has made the company fully aware of what constitutes a well balanced diet, and Heinz' commitment is reflected in the sensible nutritional advice on all their products.

Heinz has always supported the consumer's right to know about nutritional values and they were one of the first food manufacturers voluntarily to introduce full and comprehensive nutritional information panels across all products, ahead of government guidelines and legislation. Heinz nutritional information panels provide details of calorie, protein, carbohydrate, fat and fibre levels, as well as total sodium and sugars content. Values are given for an average serving in addition to amounts contained per 100g.

In the early 1980s, conscious of the effects of excessive salt and sugar, Heinz set out to reduce the levels of these ingredients in standard Heinz varieties; and to make significant reductions in added salt and sugar in the best Heinz products, since this would do most to contribute towards improving public health. Reflecting changes in consumer tastes, substantial reductions in added salt and sugar levels of up to 25 per cent have been made gradually over the last ten years. Heinz' policy of acceptable change through a careful programme of gradual salt and sugar reduction rather than massive reduction 'overnight' will continue. In this way Heinz aim to continue to contribute towards improving public health by means of good food.

There's no Taste Like Heinz

Providing food that is both tasty and enjoyable to eat is another important part of the Heinz philosophy.

Recipe creation and product development start in the experimental kitchens at the Heinz research centre. There, a team of highly trained chefs, recruited from Britain's top hotels and restaurants, use their skills to create recipes which will lose none of their subtle flavour during large-scale, computer-controlled production.

Detailed records are kept of the exact quantities used of each ingredient, at what point in the cooking it was added, and of cooking times. 'A dash of vinegar' may be all right in the home, but when a recipe is to be made on a large scale and repeated day after day, year after year, that's not good enough. Great precision and control is essential in order to ensure that each Heinz product is of consistent quality wherever and whenever it is purchased.

Apart from creating new recipes, chefs work continuously to improve existing varieties, ensuring that Heinz products remain ahead of the competition and match consumer tastes.

Using those same recipe skills, Heinz have compiled this mouthwatering selection of more than 140 recipes with some of their most popular varieties, with suggestions including quick snacks, meals for kids, salads, dishes for entertaining and nourishing main meals that the whole family will love.

Heinz Baked Beans

Ever popular, Heinz baked beans have been around in this country since 1901. Once sold as a delicacy, today Heinz sells nearly 500 million cans of baked beans every year. The beans we know have an ancient and varied history. First eaten nearly 9,000 years ago, they have been put to many uses since. In the Middle Ages, for example, crushed beans and garlic were believed to cure colds and coughs.

Today we eat baked beans for more simple reasons. They taste delicious, are full of fibre and are nutritional, as well as offering great value for money.

The Heinz range of beans includes Beans with Sausages, Curried Beans with Sultanas, Barbecue Beans, Italian Beans, and of course, Britain's favourite, Heinz Baked Beans.

Heinz Salad Dressings

Did you think Heinz salad cream, mayonnaise and the All Seasons range of dressings including Herb and Garlic, Yogurt and Chive and Thousand Island could only be used with salads? Then think again! Not only do they make a delicious dressing for sandwiches and baked potatoes but they also make versatile ingredients for many all-year-round recipes.

Heinz Canned Salads, Sandwich Spread, Toast Toppers and Apple Sauce

Heinz Canned Salads, including potato, vegetable, pasta and mixed bean salads, Heinz Sandwich Spread and Heinz Apple Sauce are all made with fresh quality ingredients perfectly preserved without the need for artificial additives. As meal accompaniments or for quick snacks thay are also versatile ingredients for more adventurous recipes.

Heinz Soups

Heinz began selling soup in Britain in 1910 with Cream of Tomato imported from Canada. Manufacturing in the UK began in 1930.

Heinz soups are made from the finest quality ingredients. Tomato Soup, for example, is made from specially selected tomatoes grown in Portugal, Greece, Italy and other Mediterranean countries. These are pulped and blended with water and milk powder, salt, sugar, sunflower oil and number of spices to a precise and secret Heinz recipe.

Whatever the weather or time of year, for family meals or festive occasions, try some of the recipe ideas here.

Heinz Tomato Ketchup, Pickles and Sauces

Heinz Tomato Ketchup was first made in 1876. One of the early Heinz products, it is now the largest selling ketchup in the world. It was first sold in the UK in Fortnum & Mason in 1886, but not manufactured here until 1946.

Heinz Tomato Ketchup is made from concentrated tomato purée, sugar, vinegar and a secret blend of spices. No colouring, artificial thickeners or preservatives are added. The thick consistency of the sauce is due entirely to the special Heinz cooking methods and the quantities of tomatoes used, almost 2lbs of tomatoes for every 15oz bottle of ketchup.

Heinz began producing pickle products in 1910, with much of the company's business being founded on pickles. The initial products produced by Heinz were Piccalilli, Chow Chow, Nabob, Ideal Pickle and a variety of mixed pickles. Ploughman's Pickles contains a sweet mix of caramel, sugar and treacle, blended with vinegar to produce the distinctive Heinz Ploughman's taste. Into this are folded crisp, crunchy vegetables and fruits to add just the right texture – not too thick and not too thin. Today, Heinz provide a range of pickles and sauces – perfect as meal accompaniments or ingredients to add a special flavour.

Weight Watchers from Heinz

All the family can keep in shape with help from the Weight Watchers from Heinz range of products. A whole variety of foods including a wide selection of frozen ready meals are available, all created for healthy eating.

Eating well and keeping a healthy weight make good sense for the whole family. That is why Weight Watchers from Heinz recipes have been carefully created with today's healthier eating guidelines in mind, with controlled levels of fat and fibre, sugar and salt, as well as calories. Satisfying portions offer all the taste to make healthy eating easy with Weight Watchers from Heinz.

The range includes everyday foods the family enjoy – mayonnaise, salad dressings, jams, marmalade, hard cheese, cheese singles, cheese spreads, bread and rolls, baked beans, spaghetti, rice pudding, soups, ice cream, frozen ready meals and delicious French bread pizzas, Cooking Sauces, canned Italian pasta meals, plus other products, soon to be launched.

The recipes in this book have been put together using some of the most popular Heinz varieties to show you just how versatile they can be. We hope you will enjoy such tasty dishes as Italian Tuna Bake, Spicy Bean Stuffed Tacos and Chicken Meatballs with Spaghetti. Once you have tried all these recipes, why not try creating a few of your own? All it takes is a little imagination and your favourite Heinz variety!

STUFFED LARGE MUSHROOMS

Raw mushrooms make an interesting base to this beany filling.

SERVES 2-3

Handful chopped parsley
1 x 210g can Heinz Mixed Bean Salad
3-4 large flat mushrooms, wiped
Handful curly endive
Small bunch watercress
½ yellow pepper, cut in thin strips

1. Mix the parsley into the Mixed Bean Salad.

2. Remove the stalks from the mushrooms.

3. Place some curly endive at the bottom of each mushroom.

4. Pile the Mixed Bean Salad into each mushroom.

5. Garnish with the watercress and strips of yellow pepper.

TIME: Preparation takes 5 minutes.

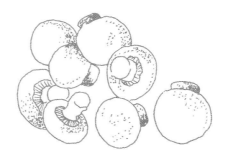

Sunny Days Soup

This makes an unusual and appetizing starter to a summer meal, and is very low in calories.

SERVES 4

120g/4oz peeled cooked prawns, chopped reserving a few for garnish
2.5cm/1in piece cucumber, peeled and diced
½ green pepper, deseeded and chopped
2 cans Weight Watchers from Heinz Mediterranean Tomato Soup
Few drops Tabasco sauce
3 tbsps natural yogurt

1. Empty Mediterranean Soup into a mixing bowl and stir in the chopped prawns, cucumber, pepper, Tabasco and yogurt.

2. Chill for about 30 minutes.

3. Serve in individual dishes garnished with the reserved whole prawns.

TIME: Preparation takes 5 minutes, and chilling requires 30 minutes.

CALORIES: 67 per serving

SERVING IDEA: Garnish with chopped fresh basil.

CRAB AND HADDOCK POTS

These delicate little pots make very smart dinner party starters.

SERVES 4

675g/1½ lbs potatoes, peeled
2 tbsps milk
15g/½ oz butter
15g/½ oz plain flour
1 x 425g can Heinz Cream of
   Asparagus Soup
Salt and freshly ground pepper
450g/1lb haddock, skinned and cut
   into chunks
1 x 170g can crabmeat, drained

---

1. Cook potatoes in boiling salted water for 20 minutes or until cooked through. Drain and mash with the milk.

2. Melt butter in a pan, add flour and cook for 1 minute.

3. Remove pan from the heat and gradually stir the Cream of Asparagus Soup into the flour and butter.

4. Return to heat and simmer gently for 2 minutes until thickened.

5. Season the sauce to taste, add the haddock and simmer for 5 minutes.

6. Stir the crab meat into the fish and sauce, and divide between 4 individual ovenproof dishes.

7. Using a piping bag fitted with a large star nozzle, pipe stars of potato on to each dish.

8. Cook at 200°C/400°F/Gas Mark 6 for 25 minutes until potato has browned.

TIME: Preparation takes 30 minutes, baking takes 25 minutes.

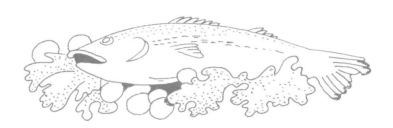

SMOKED HADDOCK CHOWDER

This thick, creamy soup is delicate in taste and sustaining in texture.

SERVES 4

1 small onion, chopped
450g/1lb potatoes, peeled and diced
2 tbsps oil
1 x 425g can Heinz Cream of Celery Soup
285ml/½ pint milk
1 bayleaf
350g/12oz smoked haddock, skinned
  and diced
1 x 198g/7oz can sweetcorn
Freshly ground black pepper
1 tbsp fresh chopped parsley

1. Gently fry onion and potatoes in oil in a large covered pan for 10 minutes.

2. Add the Cream of Celery Soup, milk and bayleaf, cover and simmer for another 10 minutes.

3. Stir in the smoked haddock and sweetcorn, season with pepper, and simmer for 5 minutes more.

4. Ladle into warmed bowls and garnish with the chopped parsley.

TIME: Preparation takes 5 minutes, cooking takes 25 minutes.

SERVING IDEA: Serve with crusty bread.

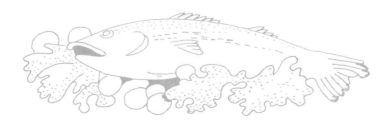

VEGETABLE AND BEEF SOUP WITH PARSLEY DUMPLINGS

This wholesome winter soup has been created for weight watchers.

SERVES 4

300ml/½ pint beef stock
2 cans Weight Watchers from Heinz
   Country Vegetable & Beef Soup

Dumplings
90g/3oz self-raising flour
1 tsp baking powder
Pinch of salt
15g/½ oz butter or margarine
4 tsps finely chopped parsley

1. Heat stock and soup together gently in a large saucepan.

2. Meanwhile, to make the dumplings, mix flour, baking powder and salt and rub in butter or margarine.

3. Stir in chopped parsley and just enough water to make a firm dough - the mixture should not be too wet.

4. Divide mixture evenly into 8 pieces and roll each between the hands to make small dumpling shapes.

5. When the soup is boiling, place the dumplings carefully on top, cover, and simmer for 10 minutes or until the dumplings are firm and well risen.

TIME: Preparation takes about 15 minutes, cooking takes 10-15 minutes.

CALORIES: 144 per serving.

CHEESY TOMATOES

*These mouthwatering savoury starters are
quick to make and good for calorie counters.*

SERVES 4

4 large tomatoes
1 tsp oil
1 small onion, chopped
60g/2oz wholemeal breadcrumbs
120g/4oz spinach, chopped finely
2 tbsps tomato purée
Pinch of nutmeg
120g/4oz Weight Watchers from Heinz
   Reduced Fat Hard Cheese, grated

1. Cut the tops off the tomatoes and scoop out the seeds.

2. Heat the oil in a small pan and sauté the onion until tender.

3. Add the breadcrumbs and fry for a few minutes.

4. Add the spinach, tomato purée and nutmeg and mix well.

5. Stir in 90g/3oz of the cheese.

6. Fill the tomato shells with the mixture, place in an ovenproof dish, cover with foil, and bake at 180°C/350°F/Gas Mark 4 for about 10 minutes.

7. Remove the foil, top with the remaining cheese and return to the oven for 5-10 minutes.

TIME: Preparation takes 15 minutes, cooking takes about 20 minutes.

CALORIES: 155 per serving.

SERVING IDEA: Serve garnished with fresh coriander leaves and shredded lettuce.

BAKED AVOCADO PEARS

This is a most unusual and irresistible avocado recipe.

SERVES 4

---

4 small avocado pears
½ x 425g can Heinz Cream of
   Chicken Soup
75g/3oz cooked chicken, chopped
100g/4oz peeled, cooked prawns
Salt and freshly ground black pepper
6 slices salami, cut into strips
25g/1oz Mozzarella cheese, grated

---

1. Cut avocado pears in half and discard stones.

2. Place on a baking tray, trimming off bases if necessary to stop them falling over.

3. In a bowl mix Cream of Chicken Soup, chicken, prawns and seasoning to taste.

4. Fill the avocados with the mixture, lay salami on top of each and sprinkle with cheese.

5. Bake at 200°C/400°F/Gas Mark 6 for 15 minutes.

TIME: Preparation takes just 5 minutes, cooking time takes 15 minutes.

SERVING IDEA: Garnish with sprigs of fresh dill.

ASSORTED DIPS WITH CRUDITÉS

These dips can be served together or separately with a variety of vegetables or crisps. They are perfect for parties or with drinks.

SERVES 6-8

Spicy cheese dip
200g/7oz skimmed milk soft cheese
3 tbsps Heinz Salad Cream
2 tsps tomato purée
1 tsp chilli sauce (adjust to taste)

Curry dip
4 tbsps Heinz Salad Cream
2 tbsps curry sauce (adjust to taste)

Avocado dip
1 large ripe avocado
1 tsp lemon juice
2 tbsps Heinz Salad Cream
Salt and freshly ground black pepper
Dash of chilli sauce

Crudités
5cm/2in lengths of celery, carrot strips,
  green and red pepper
Cauliflower and broccoli florets
Baby sweetcorn
Tortilla chips
Crisps

1. For the spicy cheese dip mix all the ingredients together. Serve in a small bowl.

2. For the curry dip mix all the ingredients together. Serve in a small bowl.

3. For the avocado dip process all ingredients in a food processor until smooth, or mash avocado with the lemon juice and then stir in the other ingredients. Serve in a small bowl.

4. Arrange the crudites on a serving platter around the dips.

TIME: Preparation takes 15 minutes.

PRAWN AND WATERCRESS COCKTAIL

This is a variation of the traditional prawn cocktail starter.

SERVES 6

225g/8oz cooked peeled prawns
Bunch of watercress, washed and
    chopped
10cm/4ins cucumber, cut in small cubes

Sauce
150ml/5fl.oz single cream
4 tbsps Heinz Salad Cream
1 tbsp tomato purée or ketchup
2 tsps lemon juice
Few shakes of Worcestershire sauce

1. Arrange a layer of watercress, prawns and cucumber in 6 glasses and put in the refrigerator to chill for about 15 minutes.

2. Mix together the sauce ingredients.

3. Just before serving, drizzle the sauce into each glass and decorate.

TIME: Preparation takes 5-10 minutes, chilling takes 10-15 minutes.

SERVING IDEA: Garnish with whole prawns, watercress and slices of lemon.

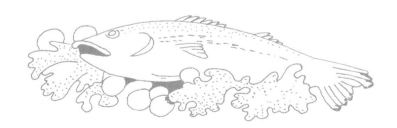

28

BEAN AND CHEESE CHOWDER

*This is a delicious creamy soup, nutritious
enough to be a light meal in itself.*

SERVES 4

25g/1oz butter or margarine
1 onion, chopped
1 clove garlic, crushed
1 x 450g/15.9oz can Heinz Baked Beans
275ml/½ pint chicken stock
150ml/¼ pint single cream
100g/4oz grated cheese
1 tbsp Worcestershire sauce
Salt and freshly ground black pepper

1. Melt the butter or margarine in a saucepan.

2. Add the onion and fry gently for 4 minutes.

3. Add the garlic, Baked Beans and chicken stock and simmer for 15 minutes.

4. Allow to cool slightly and then liquidise until smooth.

5. Return the soup to a clean pan and add the single cream and heat through gently.

6. Stir in the cheese until melted, add the Worcestershire sauce and salt and pepper to taste.

TIME: Preparation takes 5 minutes, cooking takes 30 minutes.

SERVING IDEA: Top each portion with a slice of French bread sizzling with toasted cheese and sprinkled with cayenne pepper.

BEAN STUFFED PEPPERS

These are excellent served piping hot on bonfire night.

SERVES 6

1 medium onion, finely chopped
3 tbsps oil
450g/1lb beef mince
Salt and freshly ground black pepper
1 tbsp tomato purée
150ml/¼ pint beef stock
100g/4oz button mushrooms, chopped
  or sliced
6 large, even-sized red or green peppers
2 x 450g/15.9oz cans Heinz Baked Beans
1 x 400g/14oz can tomatoes
1 clove garlic, crushed

1. Fry the chopped onion gently in the oil for 3 minutes.

2. Add the beef mince and fry until it is lightly browned.

3. Season with salt and pepper and add tomato puree, stock and mushrooms.

4. Cover and simmer for 20 minutes.

5. Meanwhile, to prepare the peppers cut a slice from each stalk end and carefully hollow out the seeds. Make sure that each pepper will stand upright, if necessary cutting a thin slice from the base without puncturing the pepper right through. Stand the hollowed peppers in a lightly greased ovenproof dish.

6. Stir the Baked Beans into the meat mixture and spoon this into the peppers.

7. Break up the canned tomatoes with a fork and mix with the garlic and a little salt and pepper, and spoon this over and around the peppers.

8. Cover with a piece of greased foil and bake at 190°C/375°F/Gas Mark 5 for 35-40 minutes. Serve hot.

TIME: Preparation takes 30 minutes, cooking takes 35-40 minutes.

EGG AND ANCHOVY PATÉ

This is a delicious combination and very quick to make.

SERVES 4

4 tbsps Heinz Mayonnaise
4 eggs, hardboiled and shelled
½ tsp anchovy purée
1 tsp capers, chopped
50g/2oz cream cheese
Freshly ground black pepper
1 tin anchovies, drained and cut into
   thin strips

1. Place all ingredients except the anchovy strips into a food processor and blend until smooth.

2. Spoon the pate into individual pots and garnish with strips of anchovy.

TIME: Preparation takes 5-10 minutes.

SERVING IDEA: Serve with melba toast.

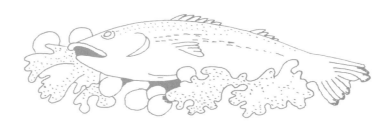

Bean Pizza Squares

*These appetizing bite-sized pizzas make a
tempting change at children's teas, and can even be
handed round with cocktails.*

SERVES 2-4

175g/6oz self-raising flour
Salt and freshly ground black pepper
40g/1½ oz butter, cut in small pieces
1 egg, beaten with 1-2 tbsps milk
Olive oil
1 x 450g/15.9oz can Heinz Baked Beans
4 tbsps sweetcorn kernels
3 tomatoes, thinly sliced
75g/3oz grated cheese

1. Sieve the flour and salt and pepper to taste into a bowl.

2. Rub in the butter finely.

3. Add the beaten egg and milk and work to a smooth dough.

4. Roll out on a floured surface to a 23cm/9in square.

5. Place on a greased baking sheet, rolling or pushing the dough out further if it shrinks when lifted.

6. Brush the dough generously with olive oil.

7. Spread the Baked Beans over the dough right to the very edge and sprinkle with the sweetcorn kernels.

8. Arrange the sliced tomatoes on top and scatter with grated cheese.

9. Bake at 220°C/425°F/Gas Mark 7 for about 25 minutes until the scone dough base has risen and the top is lightly golden.

10. Serve hot, cut into squares or fingers.

TIME: Preparation takes about 10 minutes, cooking takes 25 minutes.

COOK'S TIP: A little olive oil sprinkled over the topping during cooking prevents it from drying out. Alternatively, cover the topping with a piece of foil once it has just browned.

LAMB BURGERS WITH A SPICY PEPPER SAUCE

These chilli-laced burgers make a refreshing change from the usual fast-food variety.

SERVES 4

2 tbsps oil
1 clove garlic, crushed
2 small onions, finely chopped
1 red pepper, deseeded and finely
    chopped
7 tbsps Heinz Tomato Ketchup
4 tbsps water
½ tsp chilli powder
450g/1lb minced lamb
1 egg, beaten
Salt and freshly ground black pepper

1. Heat oil in a pan and gently fry garlic, 1 onion, pepper and chilli for 15 minutes, covered.

2. Add 4 tbsps Tomato Ketchup and water and cook for 10 minutes more.

3. In a large bowl mix together the lamb, the remaining onion and Tomato Ketchup, the beaten egg and salt and pepper to taste.

4. Form the lamb mixture into burgers and fry or grill for 6 minutes each side, or until cooked through.

5. Blend the pepper sauce in a liquidizer and serve with the burgers.

TIME: Preparation and cooking takes about an hour.

BEAN POACHER ROLLS

These unusual open-ended pasties make a tempting
and satisfying children's teatime treat.

SERVES 4

350g/12oz shortcrust pastry
2 eggs, beaten
1 x 75g/3oz packet hazelnut stuffing mix
1 x 450g/15.9oz can Heinz Baked Beans
6 small frankfurters, chopped
Salt and freshly ground black pepper
2 tbsps chopped parsley
2 tbsps grated Parmesan cheese

1. Roll out the pastry to an oblong about 40cm/16ins x 15cm/6ins and brush one of the long edges with beaten egg.

2. Make up the stuffing mix, adding only half the liquid stated on the packet, and mixing in the Baked Beans, 1 tbsp beaten egg, the chopped frankfurters, salt and pepper to taste and the chopped parsley.

3. Spoon the mixture carefully along the centre of the pastry, forming a sausage shape.

4. Lift the unglazed edge of pastry up and over the filling so that it meets the glazed edge, press edges together to seal, and notch as in the photograph.

5. Cut into four equal lengths with a sharp knife and place on a greased baking sheet.

6. Glaze with beaten egg, sprinkle with grated Parmesan cheese and bake at 190°C/375°F/Gas Mark 5 for about 30 minutes, until the pastry is golden brown. Serve straight from the oven.

TIME: Preparation takes 15 minutes, cooking takes 30 minutes.

BAKED BEAN BOATS

Push the boat out with this eye-catching recipe,
ideal for children's teas and parties.

SERVES 6

225g/8oz plain flour
1 tsp salt
75g/3oz butter or margarine
50g/2oz finely grated cheese
3-4 tbsps cold water
1 x 450g/15.9oz can Heinz Baked Beans
225g/8oz cooked turkey or chicken, diced

To serve
3 slices processed cheese, each cut into 4
   triangles
12 cocktail sticks

1. Mix the flour and salt in a bowl.

2. Rub in the fat until mixture resembles fine breadcrumbs.

3. Stir in grated cheese, then bind together with the water.

4. Leave to rest for 10 minutes.

5. Roll out and use to line 12 boat-shaped pattie tins.

6. Prick bottoms of pastry boats and chill in refrigerator for 10 minutes.

7. Bake pastry boats at 200°C/400°F/Gas Mark 6 for about 15 minutes until golden. (Keep an eye on the boats and if the pastry begins to bubble up while it is baking, flatten it gently with the back of a teaspoon.)

8. Meanwhile, heat the Baked Beans and diced turkey or chicken together in a pan.

9. Spoon the mixture into the pastry boats and top with the cheese sails secured with cocktail sticks.

TIME: Preparation takes 30 minutes, cooking time takes 15 minutes.

COOK'S TIP: Jam tart tins can be used instead of boat-shaped pattie tins.

VARIATION: For a party, add paper name pennants as in the photograph.

Jacket Potatoes with Mustard, Bacon and Mushroom Filling

This piquant filling turns the humble spud into a inviting snack or, when served with a salad, a light lunch or supper dish.

SERVES 4

4 baking potatoes, scrubbed and pricked

Filling
225g/8oz streaky bacon, cut into strips
100g/4oz mushrooms, sliced
2 tsps wholegrain mustard
6 tbsps Heinz Salad Cream

1. Bake the potatoes at 220°C/425°F/Gas Mark 7 for 1-1½ hours, or microwave for 20 minutes (650 watt setting).

2. Fry the bacon in a non-stick frying pan until crisp and golden.

3. Stir in the mushrooms and cook for a further 2-3 minutes.

4. Make a cross-wise incision in the cooked potatoes and open by pressing the base of the potatoes, and scoop out half the cooked flesh.

5. Mash together the cooked potato, bacon, mushrooms, mustard and Salad Cream.

6. Spoon the filling back into each potato and cook for a further 10 minutes in the oven or 3-4 in the microwave.

TIME: Cooking and preparation takes 1½-1¾ hours.

SERVING IDEA: Garnish with sprigs of parsley.

STUFFED PEPPERS

Sweet and exotic these stuffed peppers make a handsome lunch or supper dish.

SERVES 4

4 red peppers
450g/1lb minced beef
2 onions, chopped
½ green pepper, chopped
2 tbsps oil
5 tbsps Heinz All Seasons Herb & Garlic Dressing
50g/2oz cheese, cut into 4 slices
2 tsps ground coriander
Salt and freshly ground black pepper

1. Cut off the tops of the red peppers and deseed them.

2. Place the prepared peppers in a pan of boiling water and parboil for 2-3 minutes.

3. Fry the onion, green pepper and minced beef in the oil until the vegetables are soft.

4. Add seasoning to taste, coriander and Herb & Garlic Dressing. Mix well.

5. Fill the red peppers with the mixture, place a slice of cheese on each and bake on an ovenproof plate for 40-45 minutes at 190°C/375°F/Gas Mark 5 until the peppers are soft and the rims are beginning to brown.

TIME: Preparation takes 10 minutes, baking takes 40-45 minutes.

WESTERN BAKED ONIONS

This is a warm and spicy dish for a winter's day.

SERVES 4

4 large onions, peeled
100g/4oz streaky bacon, chopped
1 x 225g/7.9oz can Heinz Curried Beans
2 tbsps chutney
Large knob of butter

1. Place onions in a large saucepan, cover with cold water and bring to the boil.

2. Reduce heat, cover and simmer for about 30 minutes, until just tender. Drain and cool.

3. Cut a slice from each end of the onions, and remove the centre of each, leaving 2 layers as an outside wall.

4. Roughly chop 100g/4oz of the par-cooked onion.

5. Fry the chopped onion and bacon together until the bacon is crisp.

6. Stir Curried Beans and chutney into the onion and bacon mixture.

7. Stand onion 'shells' in a greased ovenproof dish, and spoon mixture into the centre of each one.

8. Dot onions with butter, add 2 tbsps water to the dish, cover with foil and bake at 200°C/400°F/Gas Mark 6 for about 30 minutes, and serve.

TIME: Preparation including boiling of onions takes 50 minutes, baking takes about 30 minutes.

SERVING IDEA: Serve with plain boiled rice.

HEINZ CURRIED SAUSAGE SALAD

This makes spicy and unusual finger food.

SERVES 4

1 x 210g can Heinz Vegetable Salad
1 tsp curry powder
8 slices cooked German sausage/salami

1. Mix together the Vegetable Salad and curry powder.

2. Place a teaspoon of the mixture on each slice of sausage and roll them up.

TIME: Preparation takes 5 minutes.

SERVING IDEA: Serve garnished with curly endive leaves.

SANDWICH SPREAD SANDWICHES

These spreads are ideal for school lunch boxes, party finger food,
quick lunches, high teas and snacks.

SERVES 4-6

Tuna and Cucumber Spread
Slice of wholemeal bread, buttered
Iceberg lettuce leaf
Heinz Cucumber Spread
2 tbsps tuna fish

Chicken and Spicy Sandwich Spread
Bridge roll, split and buttered
Slice of roast chicken
Heinz Spicy Sandwich Spread
Red lettuce leaf (lollo rosso)

Cheese and Original Sandwich Spread
Slice of red Cheddar cheese
Chunk of French stick, split and buttered
Heinz Original Sandwich Spread
Slices of tomato

Ham and Tomato and Onion Spread
Curly endive leaves
Slice of granary bread, buttered
Heinz Tomato and Onion Spread
Slice of ham

1. For the tuna and cucumber sandwich take a crusty slice of wholemeal bread and butter and place a crisp crunchy leaf of iceberg lettuce on it. Spread a layer of Cucumber Spread on the lettuce. Top with juicy chunks of tuna fish, and serve as an open sandwich.

2. For the chicken and spicy sandwich take a buttered bridge roll and lay the slice of roast chicken in the bottom. Cover the chicken with Spicy Sandwich Spread. Top the filling with a the red lettuce leaf, and close the roll.

3. For the cheese and original sandwich place the slice of cheese on the bottom half of the French bread. Spread this with a layer of Original Sandwich Spread. Top the filling with slices of tomato, and replace the top half of the bread.

4. For the ham and tomato and onion sandwich place some curly endive leaves on the slice of bread. Add a layer of Tomato and Onion Spread. Lay the slice of ham on top. Garnish with a small curly endive leaf and serve as an open sandwich.

TIME: Each sandwich takes 5 minutes to make.

PICKLE PASTIES

*Homemade pasties are beautifully moist and crumbly
straight from the oven, but are also excellent cold on picnics.*

SERVES 4

Pastry
225g/8oz plain flour
Pinch of salt
100g/4oz butter
50g/2oz Cheddar cheese, grated
4 tbsp cold water

75g/3oz each potato, carrot and leek,
  diced, cooked and cooled
4 tbsps Heinz Ploughman's Pickle
Salt and freshly ground black pepper

1. For the pastry, sift flour and salt into a bowl.

2. Rub in butter to resemble fine breadcrumbs.

3. Stir in the cheese.

4. Make a well in the centre, add the water and mix to a soft dough. Cover and chill the dough for 20 minutes.

5. Mix together the vegetables, Ploughman's Pickle and salt and pepper to taste.

6. Roll out the pastry into a large square on a lightly floured surface.

7. Using a small plate to cut round, cut out 4 circles of pastry, approximately 15cm/6ins in diameter.

8. Divide vegetable mixture into 4 and place in the centres of the pastry circles.

9. Dampen the edges of the pastry and fold up over filling to give a pasty shape. Pinch the edges together to seal.

10. Place pasties on a greased baking sheet and brush over with milk to glaze.

11. Cook at 200°C/400°F/Gas Mark 6 for 25 minutes until golden.

TIME: Preparation takes 30 minutes, cooking takes 25 minutes.

SERVING IDEA: Garnish with sprigs of parsley.

MUFFIN TOPPERS

This bacon and egg recipe would make a substantial brunch dish.

SERVES 2-4

4 round bacon steaks
2 muffins, cut in half
1 tomato, sliced
4 eggs, beaten
1 can Heinz Savoury Pizza Toast Toppers
1 tbsp milk
Salt and freshly ground black pepper

1. Cook bacon steaks under a preheated grill for 6 minutes, turning over half way through cooking.

2. Lightly grill the muffins and tomato.

3. Blend together the eggs, Savoury Pizza Toast Toppers, milk and seasoning.

4. Pour the eggs into a pan and cook, stirring, until scrambled.

5. Serve each muffin half topped with a slice of bacon, scrambled egg and a slice of tomato.

TIME: Preparation and cooking takes 10-15 minutes.

SERVING IDEA: Serve garnished with sprigs of parsley.

SOUFFLÉ POTATOES

This recipe turns baked potatoes into a very presentable meal.

SERVES 2

2 large baking potatoes
1 can Heinz Curried Chicken Toast
    Toppers
25g/1oz butter
4 spring onions, trimmed and chopped
2 eggs, separated
Salt and freshly ground black pepper

1. Prick potatoes all over with a fork.

2. Place potatoes on a baking tray and cook at 200°C/400°F/Gas Mark 6 for 1 hour 15 minutes or until cooked through.

3. Cut each cooked potato in half and scoop the insides out into a bowl, returning the skins to the baking tray.

4. Mash the potato and mix in the Curried Chicken Toast Toppers, butter, spring onions, egg yolks and seasoning.

5. Beat egg whites until stiff and gently fold into the potato mixture.

6. Spoon soufflé mixture into the potato skins and return them to the oven for 20 minutes until risen.

7. Serve immediately.

TIME: Cooking takes 2 hours.

FLYING SAUCERS

These are quick to make and fun to eat.

SERVES 4

8 large open cup mushrooms, wiped
4 spring onions, trimmed and chopped
1 tomato, skinned, deseeded and chopped
50g/2oz butter
1 can Heinz Ham and Cheese Toast
    Toppers
2 tsps chopped parsley
15g/½ oz fresh white breadcrumbs
Salt and freshly ground black pepper
Rounds of fried bread or toast to serve

1. Trim mushroom stems level with caps and chop stems finely.

2. Fry the stems, spring onions and tomato in half the butter for 3 minutes.

3. Remove from the heat and stir in the Ham and Cheese Toast Toppers, parsley, breadcrumbs and seasoning.

4. Melt the remaining butter and brush this over the domes of the mushrooms.

5. Grill the mushrooms, domes uppermost, under a preheated grill for 2 minutes.

6. Turn mushroom caps over, fill with the stuffing and return to the grill.

7. Cook under grill until the stuffing is heated through.

8. Place on fried bread or toast and serve.

TIME: Preparation and cooking take 15 minutes.

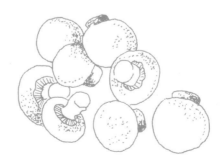

HAM AND CHEESE ROLL-UPS

These make delicious party fare, even suitable for weight watchers.

SERVES 4

4 x 30g/1oz slices ham, cut in half
Prepared mustard
4 slices Weight Watchers from Heinz
　　Reduced Fat Processed Cheese,
　　cut in half
2 eggs, hard-boiled and shelled
4 tsps Weight Watchers from Heinz
　　Reduced Calorie Dressing
Lettuce leaves, tomato and cucumber to
　　serve

1. Spread each piece of ham with mustard.

2. Arrange a slice of cheese on each slice of ham.

3. Mash the hard-boiled eggs with the Reduced Calorie Dressing.

4. Divide the egg mixture into 8 and spread over each slice of ham and cheese.

5. Roll up the ham pieces and secure with cocktail sticks.

6. Arrange the ham rolls on a bed of lettuce, and garnish with tomato and cucumber.

TIME: Preparation takes 10-15 minutes.

CALORIES: 135 per serving.

TOASTED CHEESE AND APPLE ROLLS

This makes a good vegetarian weight watchers' lunch or supper.

SERVES 4

1 onion, thinly sliced
1 dessert apple, peeled, cored and sliced
4 x 60g/2oz soft rolls
4 tsps butter or margarine
4 slices Weight Watchers from Heinz
    Reduced Fat Processed Cheese
4 tsps Weight Watchers from Heinz
    Reduced Sugar Marmalade

1. Divide the apple and onion slices into 4 portions.

2. Halve and butter the rolls.

3. Place ½ cheese slice on bottom half of each roll, then 1 portion of onion and ½ portion of the apple. Top with another ½ slice cheese, 1 tsp Marmalade and the remaining apple slices.

4. Place the tops of the rolls on the bottoms.

5. Place each roll on a large piece of foil and fold to make a parcel, leaving plenty of air space inside.

6. Bake at 190°C/375°F/Gas Mark 5 for 20 minutes.

TIME: Preparation takes 10 minutes, baking takes 20 minutes.

CALORIES: 284 per serving.

SERVING IDEA: Serve with a mixed salad.

PEPE'S PEPPER OMELETTE

This is an interesting baked omelette of Spanish origin.

SERVES 4

1 small green pepper
1 small red pepper
6 eggs
Salt and freshly ground black pepper
2 tsps oil
1 x 425g can Heinz Cream of Celery Soup
1 tbsp fresh chopped basil

1. Cook green and red peppers in boiling water for 5 minutes.

2. Drain, cool, deseed, and chop the peppers, keeping the colours separate.

3. Beat 3 of the eggs with 3 tsps water and salt and pepper to taste.

4. Heat half the oil in an omelette pan and add the green pepper and half the beaten egg.

5. Fry gently until egg has set. Carefully remove and put to one side.

6. Repeat steps 4 and 5 with the red pepper and the remaining beaten egg.

7. Beat the other 3 eggs with the Cream of Celery Soup and chopped basil.

8. Pour one third of the egg and soup mixture into a lightly oiled 15cm/6in soufflé dish.

9. Place green pepper omelette on top.

10. Repeat steps 8 and 9 using the red pepper omelette.

11. Pour the remaining third of egg and soup mixture on top.

12. Cook at 200°C/400°F/Gas Mark 6 for 40-45 minutes until set.

13. Serve hot or cold.

TIME: Preparation takes 15-20 minutes, baking takes 40-45 minutes.

SERVING IDEA: Garnish with a sprig of fresh basil.

SPICY MARROW BOATS

This flavoursome stuffed marrow makes an attractive family dish.

SERVES 4

1 small onion, chopped
1 clove garlic, crushed
225g/8oz minced beef
100g/4oz white rice
1 tbsp oil
1 x 435g can Heinz Mulligatawny Soup
Salt and freshly ground black pepper
1 tomato, skinned and chopped
1 x 432g/15.25oz can red kidney
   beans, drained
1.5-1.8kg/3½ -4lb marrow
100g/4oz Cheddar cheese, grated
Handful fresh chopped coriander

1. Fry onion, garlic, mince and rice in oil for 5 minutes.

2. Add soup and season to taste.

3. Cover and simmer for 20 minutes.

4. Stir in tomato and kidney beans and cook for a further 5 minutes until rice is tender.

5. Cut marrow in half lengthways, and scoop out seeds with a spoon.

6. Fill centres of marrow with the stuffing, and wrap each half in oiled foil.

7. Place on a baking tray and cook at 180°C/350°F/Gas Mark 4 for 1 hour.

8. Open out foil, sprinkle cheese over the top and cook for a further 15 minutes.

9. Serve garnished with chopped coriander.

TIME: Preparation takes 35 minutes, baking takes 1¼ hours.

CHEESE AND BEAN SHORTCAKE

*This savoury shortcake can be eaten hot or cold
and is a wholesome vegetarian dish.*

SERVES 6-8

225g/8oz self-raising flour
Salt
50g/2oz butter
50g/2oz finely grated cheese
6 tbsps milk
1 egg, beaten
1-2 tbsps grated Parmesan cheese

Filling
175g/6oz cream cheese, softened
1 small onion, grated
2 x 225g/7.94oz cans Heinz Curried Beans

1. Sieve the flour and salt into a bowl and rub in the butter and mix in the grated cheese.

2. Add the milk and mix to a soft dough.

3. Divide the dough into two and roll each half into a thin circle about 20cm/ 8ins in diameter.

4. Place each one on a greased baking sheet, and mark one circle into 6 or 8 segments with a sharp knife.

5. Brush both circles with the beaten egg and sprinkle with the Parmesan cheese.

6. Bake at 220°C/425°F/Gas Mark 7 for about 15 minutes, until lightly risen and golden.

7. Cut along the marked divisions on the one circle while it is still warm, and allow both circles to cool.

8. Spread the complete circle of shortcake with the cream cheese mixed with grated onion and salt and pepper to taste, and spread the Heinz Curried Beans over this.

9. Arrange the sections of shortcake on the top. Serve either cold, cut through into wedges, or wrap the assembled shortcake in foil and warm through in a moderate oven. (The cheese will soften, but it gives the shortcake a deliciously sticky texture.)

TIME: Preparation and baking of the shortcake takes 30 minutes, warming through – if required takes 10 minutes.

VARIATION: Add chopped crispy bacon, ham or cooked chicken to the cream cheese and Curried Bean filling.

TAGLIATELLE WITH CREAMY MUSHROOM SAUCE

*This rich vegetarian pasta dish is another recipe where
Salad Cream has been successfully incorporated into a hot dish
to give a beautiful creamy result.*

SERVES 4

375g/13oz tagliatelle

Sauce
1 onion, finely chopped
2 tbsps oil
350g/12oz mushrooms, sliced
150ml/5fl.oz single cream
150ml/¼ pint milk
5 tbsps Heinz Salad Cream
1 tbsp chopped parsley

1. Fry the onion in the oil until soft.

2. Stir in the mushrooms and cook for a further 5 minutes.

3. Add the cream, milk and Salad Cream, cover and cook gently for 10 minutes.

4. Cook the tagliatelle 'al dente', drain and toss with the mushroom sauce.

5. Serve piping hot, topped with chopped parsley.

TIME: Preparation takes 20-25 minutes.

VARIATION: Use spaghetti instead of tagliatelle.

BARBECUE BEAN SALAD

*Here the smoky flavour of the Barbecue Beans
echoes the flavour of the smoked chicken in this refreshing
and nourishing summer salad.*

SERVES 4-6

1 small head endive
2 x 450g/15.9oz cans Heinz Barbecue
    Beans
4 spring onions, shredded into strips
1 large red pepper, deseeded and finely
    chopped
225g/8oz boned smoked chicken (or
    ordinary cooked chicken) cut into strips
2 limes
4 tbsps olive oil
Salt and freshly ground black pepper
Handful of tortilla or potato chips,
    coarsely crushed

1. Arrange the washed endive leaves in a
shallow bowl.

2. Drain the Barbecue Beans to remove
some of the excess juice.

3. Spoon the Barbecue Beans on to the
endive, and scatter spring onion, red
pepper, and strips of chicken over the top.

4. Mix the juice from one of the limes with
the olive oil and salt and pepper to taste,
and spoon this dressing evenly over the
salad.

5. Scatter the tortilla chips on top and
garnish with wedges cut from the second
lime.

TIME: Preparation takes about 15 minutes.

MACKEREL AND HORSERADISH SALAD

*This makes a delicious and quick cold lunch, and
also is an excellent sandwich filling.*

SERVES 4

225g/8oz smoked mackerel, skinned
   and flaked
2 sticks celery, chopped
4 spring onions, finely chopped
4 tbsps Heinz Salad Cream
1 tbsp creamed horseradish sauce
Freshly ground black pepper
Chopped parsley

1. Mix together the mackerel, celery and spring onions in a bowl.

2. Stir in the Salad Cream, horseradish sauce and parsley and season with black pepper.

TIME: Preparation time is 5-10 minutes.

SERVING IDEA: Serve piled on a bed of lettuce with slices of brown bread and butter.

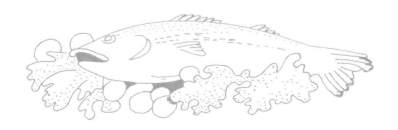

MEXICAN KEBABS

To warm up long cold winter evenings try this
easy-to-prepare spicy recipe.

SERVES 4

4 tbsps Heinz Mayonnaise
½ -1 tsp chilli powder, adjust to taste
1 tbsp lemon juice
450g/1lb lean lamb, cut into 2.5cm/
    1in cubes
100g/4oz button mushrooms, wiped
2 small onions, quartered

1. Blend together the Mayonnaise, chilli powder and lemon juice.

2. Put the meat, mushrooms and onions in a bowl and stir in the Mayonnaise mixture thoroughly.

3. Cover and leave to marinate in a cool place for at least 2 hours.

4. Thread meat, mushrooms and onions on to 4 skewers.

5. Place under a preheated grill for 15-20 minutes, turning frequently until cooked through.

TIME: Preparation takes 5 minutes, standing time is 2 hours, and cooking time is 15-20 minutes.

SAVOURY BEAN CRUMBLE

*This appetizing lunch or teatime dish is very quick to
assemble and would be excellent served with a green salad.*

SERVES 4

1 tsp oil
1 onion, finely sliced
2 sticks celery, sliced
1 small red pepper, deseeded and
chopped
2 x 225g/7.94oz cans Heinz Curried Beans
1 tbsp parsley, finely chopped
25g/1oz plain crisps, crushed
50g/2oz hard cheese, grated
25g/1oz butter

1. Heat the oil and fry the onion, celery
and pepper for a few minutes.

2. Add the Curried Beans and parsley,
mixing well together.

3. Transfer the mixture to an ovenproof
dish and sprinkle the crisps and cheese on
top.

4. Dot with butter and bake at 180°C/
350°F/Gas Mark 4 for about 30 minutes
until the topping is crisp and brown.

TIME: Preparation takes 5-10 minutes, baking takes 30 minutes.

Heinz Bohemian Salad

This instant recipe is a great standby for a quick salad lunch.

SERVES 2-4

1 tbsp German mustard
1 x 210g can Heinz Potato Salad
Handful shredded white cabbage
4 large frankfurters, sliced

1. Stir the mustard into the Heinz Potato Salad in a large salad bowl.

2. Carefully fold in the shredded cabbage and the frankfurter slices.

TIME: Preparation takes 5 minutes.

HEINZ LAYERED SALAD

This is a lovely fresh salad recipe you can throw together in minutes.

SERVES 4-6

¼-½ lettuce, shredded
50g/2oz mushrooms, wiped and sliced
1 x 210g can Heinz Vegetable Salad
4 spring onions, chopped
2 eggs, hard-boiled and chopped
100g/4oz mild Cheddar cheese, grated
100g/4oz crispy fried bacon or ham,
   cut in strips
2-3 tomatoes, thinly sliced

1. Place the shredded lettuce at the bottom of a deep glass salad bowl.

2. Scatter the mushroom slices on to the lettuce, followed by the Vegetable Salad, chopped spring onions, hard-boiled eggs, grated cheese, and then the cooked bacon or ham strips.

3. Decorate with the tomato slices, and serve.

TIME: Preparation takes 5-10 minutes.

SPAGHETTI WITH MORTADELLA HAM

This is based on a classic recipe, but made extra creamy
with the addition of the chicken soup.

SERVES 4

275g/10oz spaghetti
225g/8oz button mushrooms, wiped
  and sliced
25g/1oz butter
1 bunch spring onions, trimmed
  and chopped
225g/8oz mortadella ham, chopped
1 x 425g can Heinz Cream of
  Chicken Soup
Salt and freshly ground black pepper
2 eggs, beaten
2 tsps water
2 tsps oil
1 tbsp fresh chopped oregano

1. Cook spaghetti in plenty of boiling salted water for 10-12 minutes until tender, drain well.

2. Meanwhile, fry the mushrooms in the butter for 5 minutes in a large pan.

3. Add the spring onions, ham, Cream of Chicken Soup and seasoning to taste.

4. Stir in the spaghetti and heat through.

5. Beat eggs with the water.

6. Heat the oil in an omelette pan, add eggs and cook as an omelette over a gentle heat until cooked through.

7. Roll up omelette and slice thinly.

8. Serve spaghetti topped with the omelette slices and chopped oregano.

TIME: Preparation takes 20 minutes.

SPICY BEAN STUFFED TACOS

This makes an interesting vegetarian dish with a bite.

SERVES 2

1 tsp chilli powder
2 drops Tabasco sauce
1 x 210g can Heinz Mixed Bean Salad
2 taco shells
Slice of iceberg lettuce, shredded
2 tomatoes, diced
2.5cm/1in piece cucumber, diced

1. Mix the chilli powder, Tabasco sauce and Mixed Bean Salad together in a bowl.

2. Place a spoon of the spicy Mixed Bean Salad in the bottom of each taco shell and then layer on some lettuce, tomato and cucumber, and serve.

TIME: Preparation takes 5 minutes.

Pasta Niçoise

This is an appetizing, high-protein recipe for the salad table.

SERVES 2-4

Handful of baby sweetcorn
1 x 200g/7oz can tuna
1 x 210g can Heinz Pasta Salad
1 tomato, thinly sliced

1. Blanch the baby sweetcorn in boiling water for 1 minute, drain, cool and mix with the tin of drained tuna fish.

2. Arrange on a plate and top with the Pasta Salad.

3. Garnish with the tomato slices.

Time: Preparation takes 5-10 minutes.

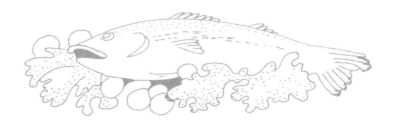

TEXAN RIBS

This juicy spare rib recipe is very easy and most effective.

SERVES 4

Marinade
1 x 435g can Heinz Cream of Tomato
Soup
1 onion, chopped
Juice of ½ orange
2 tbsps Worcestershire sauce
1 tbsp vinegar
1 tsp dry mustard powder
Salt and freshly ground black pepper

900g/2lbs spare ribs

1. Mix together the marinade ingredients, seasoning to taste.

2. Place spare ribs in a roasting tin, and pour the marinade over them, coating thoroughly.

3. Cover and leave to marinate in a cool place for 2 hours, stirring occasionally.

4. Cook ribs, uncovered, at 200°C/400°F/ Gas Mark 6 for 1 hour 15 minutes, turning over occasionally.

TIME: Preparation takes 5 minutes, marinading takes 2 hours, cooking takes 1¼ hours.

SERVING IDEA: Serve with rice and a green salad.

Tuna and Chickpea Salad

This is a really delicious combination, very quick to assemble, and suitable for the calorie conscious.

SERVES 4

198g/7oz can tuna in brine, drained
450g/15oz can chickpeas, drained
1 green pepper, deseeded and sliced
2 large tomatoes, chopped
1 tbsp mild Spanish onion, finely sliced
1 tsp capers
8 black olives, stoned and halved
4 dried apricots, chopped
3 tbsps Weight Watchers from Heinz
   Reduced Calorie Mayonnaise

1. Combine all the ingredients in a salad bowl.

2. Chill for 30 minutes and serve.

TIME: Preparation takes 10 minutes, chilling takes 30 minutes.

CALORIES: 225 per serving.

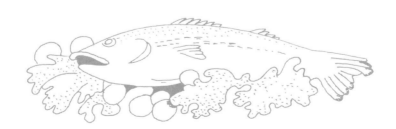

PASTA PRONTO

*This quick and appetising pasta dish is ideal for students,
single people, latecomers or anyone else eating alone.*

SERVES 1

150g/6oz green tagliatelli
½ small onion, chopped
1 clove garlic, crushed
15g/½ oz butter
1 courgette, sliced
1 can Heinz Mushroom and Bacon
    Toast Toppers
Salt and freshly ground black pepper
1 tbsp grated Parmesan cheese
2 tbsps single cream

1. Cook pasta in plenty of boiling salted
water for 6-8 minutes or according to
packet instructions.

2. Gently fry the onion and garlic in butter
for 2 minutes.

3. Add the sliced courgette and cook for 3
minutes.

4. Stir in Mushroom and Bacon Toast
Toppers.

5. Drain pasta, add to pan and mix well,
heating through.

6. Season with salt and pepper, and
transfer the pasta to a hot plate.

7. Sprinkle the pasta with Parmesan
cheese, drizzle cream over the top, and
serve.

TIME: Preparation and cooking takes 20 minutes.

Savoury Pancake Bake

*These pancake rolls, made from storecupboard ingredients,
can be prepared some time in advance of baking.*

SERVES 4

100g/4oz plain flour
Pinch of salt
1 egg, beaten
285ml/½ pint milk
Oil for frying
2 cans Heinz Chicken and Mushroom
    Toast Toppers
1 x 213g/7.5oz can red kidney beans,
    drained
1 x 198g/7oz can sweetcorn, drained
Salt and freshly ground black pepper
100g/4oz Cheddar cheese, grated

1. Sift flour and salt into a bowl.

2. Make a well in the centre and add the
egg and milk.

3. Gradually draw in the flour, using a
wooden spoon, and beat well.

4. Cover and leave to stand for 1 hour.

5. Grease and heat a pancake pan, and
make 8 pancakes.

6. In a bowl mix together the Chicken and
Mushroom Toast Toppers, beans,
sweetcorn, and seasoning.

7. Divide the filling between the 8
pancakes and roll each up.

8. Place the rolls in an ovenproof dish and
sprinkle the cheese over the top.

9. Cook at 200°C/400°F/Gas Mark 6 for
20-25 minutes until cheese is bubbling.

TIME: Preparation takes 1 hour 25 minutes, cooking takes 20-25 minutes.

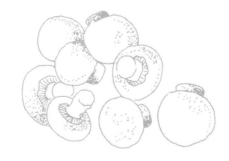

HEINZ NEPTUNE

This a another wonderfully quick lunchtime salad.

SERVES 2-4

1 x 210g can Heinz Potato Salad
1 x 200g/7oz can tuna fish
Chopped chives
Lemon juice

1. Mix the Potato Salad with the tuna fish.

2. Add a few chopped chives and a dash of lemon juice, mix well and serve.

TIME: Preparation takes 5 minutes.

SERVING IDEA: Serve in lettuce leaf shells, garnished with lemon wedges and cucumber slices.

GREEN BEAN TORTILLA

*This chunky omelette can be eaten as a lunch or
supper dish, or cut into cubes and served with drinks.*

SERVES 4

1 small onion, chopped
25g/1oz butter
150g/6oz green beans, cooked and cut
    into 2.5cm/1in lengths
6 eggs, beaten
1 can Heinz Chicken and Mushroom
    Toast Toppers
Salt and freshly ground black pepper
1 tbsp chopped chives

1. Fry onion in butter until soft.

2. Add the beans and fry for 1 minute.

3. Blend together the eggs, Chicken and
Mushroom Toast Toppers and seasoning.

4. Pour the egg mixture into an omelette
pan and cook over a low heat until just
set. Do not turn the omelette over.

5. Sprinkle the omelette with chives, cut it
into 4 pieces and serve hot or cold.

TIME: Cooking takes 10 minutes.

LIVER AND BACON PAPRIKA

*This is a high-protein lunch or supper dish,
full of flavour and rich in vitamins.*

SERVES 4

8 rashers rindless streaky bacon, each
   cut in half
1 onion, sliced
1 green pepper, deseeded and cut
   into chunks
2 tbsps oil
450g/1lb lambs' liver, thinly sliced
3 tbsps plain flour
2 tsps paprika
Salt and freshly ground black pepper
425ml/¾ pint beef stock
6 tbsps Heinz Tomato Ketchup

1. Fry bacon, onion and green pepper in
oil for 5 minutes, then remove with a
slotted spoon.

2. Coat liver in flour mixed with paprika,
salt and pepper.

3. Add floured liver to pan and quickly fry
each side to seal in juices.

4. Remove pan from heat and gradually
stir in the stock and Tomato Ketchup, then
return to the heat and bring to the boil.

5. Add the bacon mixture to the pan,
cover, and simmer for 20 minutes, stirring
occasionally.

TIME: Preparation and cooking takes 35-40 minutes.

SERVING IDEA: Serve with freshly cooked young vegetables.

SALMON AND ASPARAGUS SOUFFLÉ

*Asparagus soup adds richness and flavour
to this storecupboard recipe.*

SERVES 4

50g/2oz butter
50g/2oz plain flour
1 x 425g can Heinz Cream of
   Asparagus Soup
Freshly ground pepper
1 x 418g can red salmon
4 eggs, separated
1 extra egg white
1 tbsp fresh chopped chives

1. Melt butter in a large pan, stir in the flour and cook for 1 minute.

2. Remove pan from heat and gradually stir the Cream of Asparagus Soup into the flour and butter.

3. Return the pan to the heat, and simmer gently for 2 minutes, stirring, to give a very thick sauce.

4. Add pepper to taste, the salmon and any juice in the can, and the egg yolks.

5. Whisk all the egg whites until stiff, and carefully fold into mixture with the chives.

6. Pour into a buttered 1.4l/2½ pint soufflé dish and cook at 190°C/375°F/Gas Mark 5 for 30-35 minutes until well risen, firm to the touch and golden.

TIME: Preparation takes 10 minutes, cooking takes about 30 minutes.

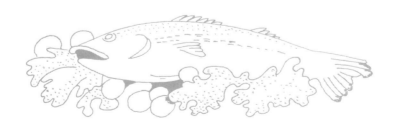

PORK AND SAUSAGE KEBABS WITH BARBECUE SAUCE

This tasty treat will be enjoyed by adults and children alike.

SERVES 4

Sauce
170ml/6fl.oz Heinz Tomato Ketchup
1 tbsp Worcestershire sauce
1 tbsp white wine vinegar
1 tbsp soft brown sugar
1 tbsp dry mustard powder
2 tsps chilli powder
Dash of Tabasco
1 clove garlic, crushed
3 tbsps oil

Kebabs
225g/8oz pork steak, cut into 2.5cm/
   1in cubes
12 mini chipolata sausages, pricked
   with a fork
8 button onions, peeled
1 red pepper, deseeded and cut into
   chunks
1 courgette, cut into 8 thick slices

1. Blend together the sauce ingredients, except the garlic and oil.

2. Gently fry the garlic in the oil for 1 minute.

3. Add the blended ingredients to the garlic and simmer for 2 minutes, then remove from the heat.

4. Thread the kebab ingredients on to long metal skewers and cook under a medium pre-heated grill for 15 minutes, turning over frequently.

5. Using a pastry brush, coat the kebabs with sauce and cook for a few minutes more, being careful not to burn them.

6. Warm through any leftover sauce and serve with the kebabs, or store in a screw-topped jar in the refrigerator for up to a week.

TIME: Preparation takes 5 minutes, cooking takes 15 minutes.

COOK'S TIP: These kebabs are even better cooked on the barbecue.

VARIATION: Simply grill the kebabs and serve the warmed sauce separately, without coating the kebabs during cooking.

DEVILLED KIDNEYS

This is a delicious and warming lunch or supper time dish.

SERVES 4

1 onion, thinly sliced
1 clove garlic, crushed
2 tbsps oil
8 lambs' kidneys, skinned and halved,
　cores removed
1 tbsp plain flour
Salt and freshly ground black pepper
4 tbsps Heinz Tomato Ketchup
140ml/¼ pint water
1 tsp dry mustard powder
½ tsp Tabasco
1 tbsp Worcestershire sauce

1. Fry onion and garlic in the oil in a large frying pan for 5 minutes.

2. Coat kidneys in the flour, seasoned with the salt and pepper.

3. Add the kidneys to the frying pan and fry for 2 minutes on each side.

4. Blend Tomato Ketchup with the water and gradually stir in to the kidneys, then bring to the boil.

5. Add mustard, Tabasco and Worcestershire sauce, and simmer for 5 minutes, turning the kidneys over frequently.

TIME: Preparation takes 5 minutes, cooking takes about 15 minutes.

SERVING IDEA: Serve on a bed of rice, garnished with triangles of fried bread and sprigs of parsley.

110

WALDORF BEAN SALAD

*This makes a crunchy and delicious summer's
lunch full of protein and vitamins.*

SERVES 4

1 x 450g/15.9oz can Heinz Barbecue
Beans
3 tbsps olive oil
Salt and freshly ground black pepper
1 clove garlic, crushed
1 tbsp chopped fresh mint
3 sticks celery, chopped
2 tbsps chopped walnuts
1 red-skinned eating apple, halved, cored
and sliced
Lemon juice
1 large lettuce heart, quartered, or 2
smaller ones, halved

1. Drain the Barbecue Beans thoroughly
in a sieve, keep the beans on one side.

2. Mix the bean juice with the olive oil,
salt and pepper to taste, the garlic and half
the chopped mint.

3. Mix the drained Barbecue Beans with
the celery, half the chopped walnuts and a
little of the dressing.

4. Arrange the lettuce hearts on a serving
dish, dip the apple slices into lemon juice
to prevent them from discolouring, and
then arrange them around the lettuce.

5. Spoon the Barbecue Bean mixture on
top of the lettuce, and pour the remaining
dressing over the top.

6. Sprinkle the salad with the remaining
chopped walnuts and mint, and serve.

TIME: Preparation takes 15 minutes.

SPINACH NOODLES

This is a quick, light and delicious pasta recipe,
suitable for the calorie conscious and vegetarians.

SERVES 2

120g/4oz noodles, e.g. tagliatelle
Salt
240g/8oz frozen leaf spinach
2-3 spring onions, roughly chopped
2 tbsps Weight Watchers from Heinz Dairy
  Spread with Cheese
2 eggs
15g/½ oz Parmesan cheese, finely grated

1. Cook the noodles in boiling salted water according to the packaging instructions.

2. Cook the spinach according to the packaging instructions, then drain well to remove all the excess water.

3. Process the drained spinach, spring onions, Dairy Spread with Cheese and eggs in a blender or food processor to form a smooth puree.

4. Drain the noodles, return them to the pan, pour the spinach puree on top and mix well.

5. Cook over a low heat, stirring all the time, until the eggs have thickened the puree.

6. Serve the noodles on two warmed plates and sprinkle with Parmesan cheese.

TIME: Preparation and cooking takes about 20 minutes.

CALORIES: 420 per serving.

COOK'S TIP: 480g/1lb fresh spinach may be used in place of the frozen variety. Wash the leaves, shake to remove excess water then place in a pan, cover and cook for 5-6 minutes until wilted.

BROCCOLI BAKE

*This easy low-calorie recipe makes a
good lunch or supper dish.*

SERVES 4

720g/1lb 8oz broccoli
1 x 295g can Weight Watchers from
    Heinz Chicken Soup
2 tsps cornflour
1 tsp dried tarragon
Salt and freshly ground black pepper
4 slices Weight Watchers from Heinz
    Reduced Fat Processed Cheese Singles
8 tsps dry breadcrumbs
4 tsps grated Parmesan cheese
½ tsp mustard powder
¼ tsp paprika

1. Cook broccoli in boiling salted water
until just tender and drain well.

2. Meanwhile, heat Chicken Soup gently
in a pan.

3. Mix cornflour with 1 tbsp water and stir
into the soup with the tarragon and salt
and pepper to taste.

4. Bring to the boil and simmer, stirring,
for 3-4 minutes.

5. Arrange drained broccoli in a shallow
ovenproof dish, pour on the soup mixture,
and lay the Cheese Slices on top.

6. Mix the breadcrumbs, Parmesan,
mustard powder and paprika and sprinkle
evenly over the dish.

7. Bake at 190°C/375°F/Gas Mark 5 for 15-
20 minutes until lightly browned.

TIME: Preparation takes 20 minutes, and baking takes 20 minutes.

CALORIES: 145 per serving.

SAVOURY BREAD AND BUTTER PUDDING

This is a high-protein supper dish that is easy to prepare in advance.

SERVES 4

40g/1½ oz butter
8 slices bread, crusts removed
2 tomatoes, skinned and sliced
6 rashers back bacon, grilled and chopped
75g/3oz Cheddar cheese, grated
Freshly ground black pepper
1 x 425g can Heinz Cream of Celery Soup
2 eggs, beaten

1. Butter bread and cut each slice into 4 triangles.

2. Place a layer of bread, buttered side up, in the bottom of a buttered ovenproof dish.

3. Arrange one of the sliced tomatoes, half the bacon and a third of the cheese over the bread, and season with pepper.

4. Repeat layers, finishing with a layer of bread, then cheese.

5. Blend soup and eggs together, then pour all over the dish easing the liquid down through the layers with a fork.

6. Cook at 190°C/375°F/Gas Mark 5 for 40 minutes until golden.

TIME: Preparation takes 15 minutes, baking takes 40 minutes.

NOODLES WITH BEAN SAUCE

*Beans and noodles make a surprisingly good match for
one another, and this is a colourful, inviting dish.*

SERVES 4

350g/12oz green noodles
1 tsp salt
2 tbsps oil
4 spring onions, chopped
4 rashers lean bacon, cut into strips
1 clove garlic, crushed
Freshly ground black pepper
1 x 450g/15.9oz can Heinz Baked Beans
Grated Parmesan cheese

1. Lower noodles into a large pan of
rapidly boiling salted water, and cook
until just tender.

2. Meanwhile, heat the oil in a pan and
add the white parts of the chopped spring
onions (reserving the green parts for
garnish), the bacon, garlic, and salt and
pepper to taste.

3. Fry lightly for 3-4 minutes.

4. Stir in the Baked Beans and heat
through.

5. Drain the cooked noodles and pile into
a warmed serving dish.

6. Top with the hot Baked Bean and
bacon sauce and garnish with the
chopped green spring onion.

7. Serve immediately, accompanied by
grated Parmesan cheese.

TIME: Preparation takes 5 minutes, cooking takes 10-15 minutes.

CHINESE NOODLE STIR-FRY

This super-quick recipe is healthy and attractive.

SERVES 4

225g/8oz egg noodles
1 tbsp sesame oil
1 tbsp chopped ginger root
100g/4oz mangetout, trimmed and sliced
100g/4oz baby sweetcorn, halved
  lengthways
1 red pepper, deseeded and cut into
  chunks
1 onion, cut into chunks
100g/4oz Chinese leaves, shredded
100g/4oz bean sprouts
1 x 425g can Heinz Cream of
  Mushroom Soup
2 tbsps light soy sauce
Salt and freshly ground black pepper

1. Place noodles in a large bowl.

2. Pour plenty of boiling water over the noodles and leave to stand for 6 minutes. Drain well.

3. Heat oil in a very large pan or wok.

4. Add ginger, mangetout, sweetcorn, pepper and onion, and stir fry for 5 minutes until sweetcorn begins to soften.

5. Add rest of ingredients and bring to the boil.

6. Stir in noodles and heat through.

TIME: Preparation and cooking of this dish takes 15 minutes.

SERVING IDEA: Include this in a spread of various Chinese dishes.

Eggs Florentine

This is a simple, light supper dish - the classic marriage of eggs and spinach given extra appeal with creamy asparagus soup.

SERVES 4

450g/1lb frozen whole leaf spinach, defrosted
Salt and freshly ground black pepper
4 eggs
½ x 425g can Heinz Cream of Asparagus Soup
50g/2oz Gruyère cheese, grated
½ tsp cayenne pepper

1. Cook spinach in a little boiling water for 3 minutes, drain well and squeeze out excess liquid.

2. Season the spinach to taste and arrange in a heatproof dish making 4 wells for the eggs.

3. Poach eggs in boiling water, drain and place in the spinach wells.

4. Pour the Cream of Asparagus Soup over the eggs, leaving a rim of spinach uncovered around the edge.

5. Sprinkle cheese and cayenne over the soup and cook under a preheated grill until cheese is bubbling and beginning to brown. Serve.

TIME: Preparation and cooking takes 10-15 minutes.

TUNA SALAD ROYALE

*This delicious and colourful fishy salad is spiced
and filled out with Curried Beans and makes a very
satisfying summer supper dish.*

SERVES 4

1 head radicchio (red lettuce)
1 cos lettuce heart
2 x 225g/7.94oz cans Heinz Curried Beans
1 x 200g/7oz can tuna in brine, drained
8 button mushrooms, thinly sliced
2 hard boiled eggs
4 anchovy fillets (optional)
1 tbsp chopped chives
Juice of ½ lemon
3 tbsps olive oil
Salt and freshly ground black pepper

1. Separate the leaves of the radicchio,
wash and shake dry and arrange on a
large salad platter.

2. Cut the lettuce heart into quarters, wash
and shake dry and arrange on top.

3. Spoon the beans onto the salad in four
sections, arrange chunks of tuna on the
top, and scatter the sliced mushrooms
over this.

4. Separate the whites and yolks of the
hard boiled eggs, and chop the whites and
sieve the yolks. Sprinkle these over the
salad.

5. Mix the lemon juice and olive oil with
seasoning to taste and sprinkle over the
salad.

TIME: Preparation takes about 10-15 minutes.

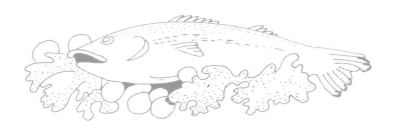

QUICK BARBECUE BEAN HOTPOT

*This is a lively outdoor casserole that can be kept
warm to one side of the smouldering barbecue coals.*

SERVES 4-6

8 plump sausages
Oil
1 large onion, thinly sliced
2 green or red peppers, deseeded
   and sliced
Generous pinch of paprika
Salt and freshly ground black pepper
1 clove garlic, crushed
2 x 450g/15.9oz cans Heinz Barbecue
   Beans

1. Brush the sausages lightly with oil, and
grill on the preheated barbecue for 4-5
minutes on each side.

2. Meanwhile, fry the onion fairly briskly
for 3-4 minutes in the oil in a frying pan.

3. Add the sliced peppers, paprika, salt
and pepper to taste and the garlic, and fry
briskly for a further 3 minutes.

4. Stir the Barbecue Beans into the onion
and pepper mixture, warm through and
put into a flameproof casserole with the
barbecued sausages. Cover, and keep
warm on the barbecue.

TIME: Preparation of this dish takes about 15 minutes.

SERVING IDEA: Serve with hot crusty bread and a tossed salad.

Chicken Meatballs with Spaghetti

This is a weight watchers' fun dish for the young.

SERVES 4

360g/12oz minced lean chicken
1 clove garlic, crushed
1 tsp crushed cardamom seeds
½ tsp ground coriander
1 tsp chopped fresh thyme
Salt and freshly ground black pepper
60g/2oz wholemeal breadcrumbs
1 egg, beaten
1 tbsp oil
1 onion, finely chopped
210ml/7fl.oz chicken stock
2 x 450g/15.9oz cans Weight Watchers
    from Heinz Spaghetti

1. Mix the minced chicken with the garlic, cardamom, coriander, thyme and a little salt and pepper to taste.

2. Add the breadcrumbs and the beaten egg.

3. Shape the mixture into small balls and chill for 30 minutes.

4. Heat the oil in a deep pan, add the onion and cook gently for 3 minutes.

5. Add the chicken balls and cook gently until sealed on all sides.

6. Pour on the stock, cover the pan and simmer gently for 10 minutes.

7. Stir in the Spaghetti and simmer gently, covered, until the chicken balls are cooked through.

TIME: Preparation and cooking takes about 45 minutes.

CALORIES: 344 per serving.

VARIATION: Use minced turkey instead of chicken.

SERVING IDEA: Serve garnished with fresh thyme or parsley.

ITALIAN LIVER

This low-calorie dish is easy to make and highly nutritious.

SERVES 4

1 onion, sliced
1 clove garlic, crushed
2 tsps oil
120g/4oz mushrooms, wiped and sliced
360g/12oz lamb's liver, sliced
2 tbsps tomato purée
¼ tsp mixed herbs
1 bayleaf
1 x 295g can Weight Watchers from
   Heinz Minestrone Soup
4 tbsps low fat natural yogurt (optional)

1. Sauté the onion and garlic in the oil in a wide, heavy-bottomed pan over medium heat for 3-4 minutes, stirring.

2. Add the mushrooms and cook for a further 4 minutes.
3. Remove the vegetables from the pan and set aside.
4. Fry the liver pieces in the pan until lightly and evenly browned.
5. Return the vegetables to the pan, adding the tomato purée, herbs, bayleaf and Minestrone Soup, heat through and simmer for 10-15 minutes until the liver is tender.
6. Transfer to a serving dish and carefully pour the yogurt over the liver.

TIME: Cooking takes about 30 minutes.

CALORIES: 217 per serving.

SERVING IDEA: Serve garnished with finely chopped parsley and accompanied by a green salad.

BEEF AND TOMATO CURRY

This is a good traditional curry dish, warming and revitalising.

SERVES 4

1 large onion, sliced
1 clove garlic, crushed
2.5cm/1in piece ginger root, peeled
   and chopped
3 tbsps oil
1 bayleaf
1 cinnamon stick
1 tsp crushed chillies
½ tsp cumin seeds
1 tbsp garam masala
½ tsp ground turmeric
½ tsp salt
675g/1½ lbs stewing steak, cut into
   2.5cm/1in cubes
4 tbsps Heinz Ploughman's Pickle
1 x 397g/14oz can chopped tomatoes

1. Gently fry the onion, garlic and ginger in the oil for 5 minutes.

2. Add the bayleaf, cinnamon, chillies and cumin and fry for 1 minute.

3. Stir in the garam masala, turmeric, salt and meat and cook until meat has browned on all sides.

4. Stir in the Ploughman's Pickle and tomatoes, cover, and simmer for 2 hours, stirring occasionally, until meat is tender.

5. Serve with rice.

TIME: Cooking takes 2¼ hours.

GAMMON WITH RUBY SAUCE

*Cooking gammon in this way with the sweet,
rich flavours of the tomato pickle and port, turns it
into a very special Sunday lunch dish.*

SERVES 4

1.25kg/2½ lb gammon joint
1 onion, quartered
1 carrot, peeled
1 bayleaf
Few cloves
6 tbsps Heinz Ploughman's Tomato Pickle

Sauce
½ small onion, finely chopped
140ml/¼ pint ruby port
Grated rind and juice of 1 orange
Pinch ground ginger
Salt and freshly ground black pepper
2 tsps cornflour

1. Place the gammon, skin side down, in a pan, cover with cold water and bring to the boil.

2. Discard the water and cover with fresh cold water, add the onion, carrot, bayleaf and cloves, bring to the boil and skim.

3. Cover and simmer gently for 1½ hours.

4. Remove from heat and leave to stand in the water for 15 minutes.

5. Meanwhile, to make the sauce, place 4 tbsps of the pickle in a pan and add the ½ onion, port, orange rind and juice, ginger and seasoning to taste.

6. Bring sauce to the boil and simmer for 10 minutes.

7. Mix cornflour with a little cold water, add to pan and simmer until thickened.

8. Remove gammon from pan and remove skin.

9. Coat the fat on the gammon with the remaining pickle and cook at 230°C/450°F/Gas Mark 8 for 5 minutes.

10. Serve in slices with the sauce.

TIME: Preparation and cooking take 2 hours.

SERVING IDEA: Garnish with twists of orange and sprigs of parsley.

CUMBERLAND PICKLE PIE

*This is a good, old-fashioned recipe, and if
served cold is excellent for picnics.*

SERVES 6

450g/1lb Cumberland sausage

Pastry
275g/10oz plain flour
Pinch of salt
125g/5oz butter
6 tbsps cold water

50g/2oz sage and onion stuffing mix
200ml/7fl.oz boiling water
6 tbsps Heinz Ploughman's Tomato Pickle
Milk to glaze

1. Prick sausage all over with a fork.

2. Coil sausage into a 15cm/6in sandwich cake tin and cook at 190°C/375°F/Gas Mark 5 for 30 minutes. Leave to cool.

3. Meanwhile, to make the pastry, sift flour and salt into a bowl.

4. Rub in the butter until it resembles fine breadcrumbs.

5. Make a well in the centre, add the cold water and mix to a soft dough.

6. Wrap and chill for 20 minutes.

7. Make up stuffing with boiling water and leave to stand.

8. Roll out ¾ of the pastry on a lightly floured surface and use to line a 5cm/2in deep, 18cm/7in wide, loose-bottomed, greased cake tin.

9. Place sausage in pastry case, top with the Tomato Pickle and then the stuffing, leaving 1cm/½ in pastry at the top.

10. Turn the pastry in at the top and dampen with water.

11. Roll out the remaining pastry and cover pie, pressing down edges to seal.

12. Brush over with milk and pierce a hole in top of pie to allow steam to escape.

13. Cook for 1 hour, until pastry is golden. Serve hot or cold.

TIME: Preparation takes 45 minutes, baking takes an hour.

SWEET AND SOUR FISH

This oriental, low-calorie dish is as good to look at as it is to eat.

SERVES 4

600g/1lb 4oz boned monkfish (or other firm white fish), cubed
2 tbsps soya sauce
Juice and grated rind of ½ lime
Small piece of fresh root ginger, peeled and grated
Salt and freshly ground black pepper
1 clove garlic, finely chopped
1 onion, finely chopped
1 tbsp oil
1 large carrot, grated
1 red pepper, deseeded and cut into thin strips
2 tbsps red wine vinegar
1 tbsp Weight Watchers from Heinz Apricot Reduced Sugar Jam
120ml/4fl.oz fish stock
60ml/2fl.oz tomato juice
1 x 450g/15.9oz can Weight Watchers from Heinz No Added Sugar Baked Beans
60g/2oz chopped dried apricots

1. Put the cubed fish into a shallow dish with the soya sauce, lime juice and rind, grated ginger, a little salt and pepper to taste and the garlic. Stir the cubes of fish to coat them evenly, cover and chill for 2 hours.
2. Meanwhile, cook the onion gently in the oil for 3 minutes.
3. Add the carrot, red pepper, wine vinegar, Apricot Jam, fish stock and tomato juice, cover and simmer gently for 10 minutes.
4. When the fish has been marinated sufficiently, add it with the marinade, the Baked Beans and the chopped apricots to the vegetables and stock.
5. Cover the dish, and simmer until the fish is just cooked through.
6. Serve piping hot on a bed of cooked brown rice.

TIME: Marinating requires 2 hours, extra cooking takes 10-15 minutes.

CALORIES: 303 per serving.

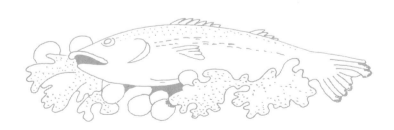

CHEESY PASTA AND VEGETABLE BAKE

This is a tempting calorie-reduced dish, suitable for all the family.

SERVES 4

60g/2oz margarine
240g/8oz leeks, washed, trimmed and
    sliced
120g/4oz mushrooms, halved
30g/1oz plain flour
300ml/½ pint chicken stock or
    skimmed milk
180g/6oz Weight Watchers from Heinz
    Reduced Fat Hard Cheese
120g/4oz pasta shapes, cooked until
    tender
Paprika

1. Melt the margarine in a saucepan, add the leeks and mushrooms and sauté for 2-3 minutes.

2. Stir in the flour and cook for 2 minutes.

3. Gradually add the stock or milk, stirring, bring to the boil and simmer for a few minutes.

4. Remove the pan from the heat and add 120g/4oz of the Reduced Fat Hard Cheese and the pasta, stirring well.

5. Pour the contents of the pan into an ovenproof dish, scatter on the remaining Reduced Fat Hard Cheese, sprinkle with paprika and bake at 180°C/350°F/Gas Mark 4 for 30 minutes until the top is browned and bubbling.

TIME: Preparation takes 15 minutes, baking takes 30 minutes.

CALORIES: 410 per serving.

SERVING IDEA: Serve garnished with watercress.

CHICKEN AND VEGETABLE PIE

This weight watchers' pie is filling and
warming on a winter's evening.

SERVES 4

1 onion, chopped
2 large carrots, thinly sliced
1 tbsp oil
480g/1lb diced chicken
1 tbsp plain flour
2 x 295g cans Weight Watchers from
    Heinz Chicken Noodle Soup
120g/4oz frozen peas
1 tbsp chopped parsley
Salt and freshly ground black pepper
720g/1lb 8oz potatoes, boiled and mashed
30g/1oz butter or margarine
3 slices Weight Watchers from Heinz
    Reduced Fat Processed Cheese Singles,
    finely chopped

1. Soften the onion and carrot in the oil
for 5 minutes.

2. Add the chicken and cook until evenly
browned.

3. Stir in the flour and cook for 1 minute.

4. Add the Chicken Noodle Soup and
peas, bring to the boil and simmer gently
for 15 minutes.

5. Beat the mashed potato with the butter
or margarine, add salt and pepper to taste,
and mix in two-thirds of the chopped
cheese.

6. Put the chicken mixture into a deep
gratin dish, and add the parsley. Fork or
pipe the potato over the top, and sprinkle
with the remaining chopped cheese.

7. Bake at 190°C/375°F/Gas Mark 5 for 25-
30 minutes.

TIME: Preparation takes 45 minutes, cooking takes 30 minutes.

CALORIES: 470 per serving.

SERVING IDEA: Serve garnished with parsley.

COOK'S TIP: Leftover cooked chicken can be used in this recipe. Make the vegetable base
and sauce and then add the chopped cooked chicken.

PORK AND BEAN STROGANOFF

*This weight watchers' recipe is equally suitable for
family meals as it is for entertaining.*

SERVES 4

1 onion, finely chopped
25g/1oz butter
1 tbsp oil
450g/1lb pork fillet, cut into thin strips
Seasoned plain flour
200ml/⅓ pint chicken stock, or dry white wine
1 clove garlic, crushed
100g/4oz button mushrooms, left whole if small, or sliced
1 tbsp chopped chives
1 x 450g/15.9oz can Weight Watchers from Heinz Baked Beans
Dry sherry and soured cream (optional)

1. Fry the onion gently in the butter and oil for 3 minutes.

2. Dust the pork strips in the seasoned flour and add them to the hot fat, and fry until sealed and lightly coloured on all sides.
3. Stir in the stock and the garlic and bring to the boil.
4. Add the mushrooms and simmer gently for 12-15 minutes, until the pork is tender.
5. Stir in the chives and Baked Beans and heat through.
6. If desired, a little dry sherry and some soured cream can be stirred into the dish immediately before serving.

TIME: Preparation and cooking takes about 35 minutes.

CALORIES: 373 per serving.

SERVING IDEA: Serve piping hot with cooked noodles or rice.

PIQUANT LAMB WITH RICE

This makes a substantial healthy meal that every member
of the family can enjoy, whether watching the calories or not.

SERVES 4

600g/1lb 4oz lamb fillet
180g/6oz onion, chopped
2 cloves garlic, crushed
2 tsps reduced fat spread
1 tsp paprika
¼ tsp ground cinnamon
½ tsp ground coriander
1 tsp ground cumin
1 tsp ground ginger
1 can Weight Watchers from Heinz Lentil
  & Carrot Soup
1 tbsp lemon juice
60g/2oz sultanas
Salt and freshly ground black pepper
240g/8oz cooked long grain rice, hot

1. Grill the lamb fillet on a rack under high heat for 5 minutes on each side.

2. Allow the meat to cool slightly, then dice into bite-sized cubes.

3. Melt the fat in a large pan and cook the onion and garlic until beginning to soften.

4. Sprinkle the spices into the pan and cook, stirring well, for 3-4 minutes.

5. Add the lamb and turn the dice in the mixture until well coated.

6. Add the Lentil & Carrot Soup, lemon juice and sultanas and bring to the boil.

7. Lower the heat and simmer for 30-40 minutes, uncovered, until lamb is tender, stirring occasionally.

8. Add salt and pepper to taste.

9. Spoon over the hot rice on a serving dish.

TIME: Preparation and cooking takes about an hour.

CALORIES: 511 per serving.

SERVING IDEA: Garnish with chopped coriander or parsley.

BACON AND SWEETCORN QUICHE

*This is a good combination for a quiche filling, the sweetcorn
giving extra bite without adding many calories.*

SERVES 6

180g/6oz plain or wholemeal pastry
2 tsps oil
1 small onion, finely chopped
120g/4oz bacon, chopped
180g/6oz sweetcorn
3 small eggs, beaten
150g/5oz natural yogurt
1 tsp mustard
120g/4oz Weight Watchers from Heinz
    Reduced Fat Hard Cheese
2 tomatoes, skinned and sliced

1. Roll out the pastry and use to line a quiche dish.

2. Line with greaseproof paper, fill with baking beans and bake blind at 200°C/400°F/Gas Mark 6 for 10-15 minutes.

3. Meanwhile, heat the oil in a saucepan and sauté the onion and bacon for about 5 minutes.

4. Add the sweetcorn and continue cooking for 2 minutes.

5. In a bowl, mix the eggs, yogurt, mustard and 90g/3oz of the Reduced Fat Hard Cheese.

6. Take the pastry out of the oven and remove the paper and baking beans.

7. Stir the egg mixture into the bacon and sweetcorn, then pour it all into the pastry case.

8. Sprinkle on the remaining Reduced Fat Hard Cheese, cut the tomato slices in half and arrange them on top.

9. Bake at 190°C/375°F/Gas Mark 5 for 30 minutes or until the top is golden and set.

TIME: Preparation takes 25-30 minutes, cooking takes 30 minutes.

CALORIES: 360 per serving.

SERVING IDEA: Garnish with a sprig of parsley.

CHICKEN WELLINGTONS

*Chicken and pickle make a light and interesting
change to the normal beef variety of Wellington.*

SERVES 4

4 chicken breasts, skinned and boned
375g/13oz pack frozen puff pastry,
　 defrosted
50g/2oz chicken liver pate
4 tbsps Heinz Ploughman's Mild
　 Mustard Pickle
1 egg, beaten

1. Cook chicken breasts at 180°C/350°F/
Gas Mark 4 for 30 minutes until cooked
through. Leave to cool.

2. Roll out pastry into a large square on a
lightly floured surface and cut into 4 equal
sized squares.

3. Make a split down one side of each
chicken breast and fill with pate.

4. Place 1 tbsp of Ploughman's Mild
Mustard Pickle in the centre of each piece
of pastry and place a chicken breast on
top of this.

5. Dampen edges of pastry with water and
fold up like a parcel. Decorate with pastry
trimmings.

6. Place the parcels on a lightly greased
baking tray, fold side down, and brush
with beaten egg.

7. Cook at 220°C/425°F/Gas Mark 7 for 25
minutes until golden.

TIME: Preparation takes 45 minutes, cooking takes 25 minutes.

SERVING IDEA: Serve with a mixed leaf salad.

LAMB STEW WITH MUSTARD DUMPLINGS

*This thick meaty stew with its mild spicy dumplings
makes a marvellously reviving dish on a wintry night.*

SERVES 6

900g/2lbs stewing lamb
150g/6oz each parsnip, turnip, onion,
    carrot, peeled and cut into chunks
25g/1oz pearl barley
25g/1oz red lentils
825ml/1½ pints lamb or chicken stock
Salt and freshly ground black pepper

Dumplings
225g/8oz self-raising flour
Pinch of salt
100g/4oz shredded suet
1 tbsp chopped parsley
4 tbsps Heinz Ploughman's Mild
    Mustard Pickle
85ml/3fl.oz water

1. Place lamb, vegetables, barley and
lentils in a large pan.

2. Add stock to pan and season with salt
and pepper.

3. Bring the stock to the boil, cover and
gently simmer for 2 hours, stirring
occasionally.

4. For the dumplings, sift flour and salt
into a bowl.

5. Stir the suet, parsley and Ploughman's
Mild Mustard Pickle into the flour.

6. Make a well in the centre of the bowl,
add the water and mix to a fairly dry
dough.

7. Form the dough into 6 dumplings and
add to the stew.

8. Cover the pan and cook for 25 minutes
until the dumplings are cooked through.

TIME: Cooking takes 2 hours 45 minutes.

PORK WITH APPLE AND PICKLE STUFFING

Here, piccalilli marries well with the classic partners pork and apple.

SERVES 4

Stuffing
2 tbsps Heinz Ploughman's Piccalilli
50g/2oz fresh white breadcrumbs
½ small onion, finely chopped
100g/4oz cooking apple, peeled, cored
  and grated
25g/1oz shredded suet
1 tsp dried sage
Salt and freshly ground black pepper
1 tbsp milk

900g/2lbs rolled belly of pork
Salt

1. Mix together all the stuffing ingredients.

2. Untie the belly of pork and place the stuffing in the centre.

3. Roll up the meat and re-tie with string.

4. Place the stuffed pork in a roasting tin and rub a little salt into the skin to make crackling.

5. Cook at 180°C/350°F/Gas Mark 4 for 2 hours until juices run clear when a skewer is inserted.

TIME: Preparation takes 10 minutes, cooking takes 2 hours.

SERVING IDEA: Serve on a fresh crunchy bed of curly endive.

HAM AND PICKLE QUICHE

The tangy crunchiness of piccalilli gives an interesting bite to quiche which is always popular summer or winter, lunch or dinner.

SERVES 6

Pastry
225g/8oz wholemeal plain flour
Pinch of salt
100g/4oz butter
4 tbsps cold water

225g/8oz ham, roughly chopped
4 tbsps Heinz Ploughman's Piccalilli
285ml/½ pint milk
3 eggs, beaten
Salt and freshly ground black pepper
1 tomato, sliced

1. To make the pastry, sift flour and salt into a bowl.

2. Rub butter into the flour to resemble fine breadcrumbs.

3. Make a well in the centre, add the water and mix to a soft dough.

4. Wrap and chill the dough for 20 minutes.

5. Roll out pastry dough on a lightly floured surface, and line a 23cm/9in flan dish.

6. Prick base lightly with a fork, line with foil or greaseproof paper, fill with baking beans and bake blind at 190°C/375°F/Gas Mark 5 for 15 minutes.

7. Remove from oven and leave to cool.

8. Spread the ham out in the pastry case.

9. Blend Piccalilli, milk, eggs, and salt and pepper together, and then pour over the ham.

10. Arrange the tomato slices on top and bake at 190°C/375°F/Gas Mark 5 for 40 minutes until set.

TIME: Preparation takes an hour, cooking takes 40 minutes.

SERVING IDEA: Eat hot or cold with cooked vegetables or salad.

Beef and Potato Savoury

Attractive and versatile, this pie makes a good family dish.

SERVES 4

675g/1½ lbs potatoes, peeled
450g/1lb minced beef
1 onion, chopped
6 tbsps Heinz Ploughman's Sandwich
 Pickle
50g/2oz fresh white breadcrumbs
2 eggs, beaten
½ tsp salt
Freshly ground black pepper
25g/1oz butter

1. Parboil the potatoes for 8 minutes, drain and allow to cool.

2. Slice the cooled potatoes thinly.

3. Mix together the remaining ingredients in a bowl.

4. Press half the meat mixture into a lightly greased round 23cm/9in-diameter ovenproof dish or tin.

5. Cover the meat with half the potato slices.

6. Add a layer of the remaining meat, and then the remaining potatoes.

7. Dot butter over the potatoes and bake at 190°C/375°F/Gas Mark 5 for 1 hour.

8. Serve hot or cold cut into wedges.

TIME: Preparation takes 20 minutes, cooking takes an hour.

STEAK WITH MUSHROOM AND BACON SAUCE

*This quick and simple sauce turns steak
into a really special dinner.*

SERVES 2

1 tbsp oil
2 sirloin steaks
1 can Heinz Mushroom and Bacon Toast
  Toppers
6 tbsps single cream
1 tsp English mustard
1 tsp capers, chopped
Salt and freshly ground black pepper
1 tbsp chopped parsley

1. Heat oil in a frying pan, and fry steaks
quickly for a few minutes each side
according to taste. Remove them from the
pan and keep hot.

2. Add Mushroom and Bacon Toast
Toppers, cream, mustard and capers to
juices in pan and heat through.

3. Season the sauce to taste, then pour
over steaks and sprinkle with parsley to
serve.

TIME: Preparation and cooking take about 15 minutes.

BEEF AND VEGETABLE STEAMED PUDDING

*This is a wholesome suet pudding, rather lighter in consistency
than the usual steak and kidney.*

SERVES 4

450g/1lb stewing steak, cut into 1cm/
   1/2in cubes
1 small onion, chopped
100g/4oz each carrot, swede and parsnip,
   peeled and cut into dice
2 tbsps plain flour
Salt and freshly ground black pepper

Dough
275g/10oz self-raising flour
125g/5oz shredded suet
2 tsps caraway seeds
200ml/7fl.oz water

5 tbsps Heinz Tomato Ketchup
6 tbsps water

1. Place beef and vegetables in a bowl, sprinkle in the plain flour and season to taste with salt and pepper, mix well.

2. For the dough, sift the self-raising flour with a pinch of salt into another bowl, and stir in the suet and caraway seeds.

3. Make a well in the centre of the flour, suet and seeds, add water and mix to a soft dough.

4. Knead the dough lightly and roll out on a floured surface to a 2.5cm/1in round.

5. Cut out ¼ of the round in a fan shape to within 2.5cm/1in of the centre.

6. Line a greased 1.4l/2½ pint pudding basin with the large piece of dough, pressing into the base and up the sides. The dough should overlap the basin top by about 2.5cm/1in.

7. Spoon the meat mixture into the pudding basin.

8. Mix Tomato Ketchup with the water and pour on to the meat. The liquid should come about two-thirds of the way up the meat mixture.

9. Fold the excess dough around the top of the basin inwards and dampen with water.

10. Roll out the remaining dough into a circle to fit the top of the basin, and place on top of mixture, pressing down edges to seal.

11. Cut two circles, one of foil and one of greaseproof paper, large enough to cover and overlap the basin. Make a pleat across both circles to allow for expansion of the pudding.

12. Butter one side of the greaseproof circle and place this over the pudding basin, cover with the foil circle, and tie them in place with some string.

13. Bring a large pan of water to the boil.

14. Put the pudding basin in the water which should come two-thirds of the way up the side of the basin.

15. Cover the pan with a tight-fitting lid and steam for 5 hours, topping up with boiling water when necessary.

16. To serve, uncover the basin and turn the pudding out on to a warmed plate.

TIME: Preparation takes 20-25 minutes, cooking takes 5 hours.

CHICKEN CHANA

*These spicy chicken portions on their bed of chickpeas
make a delicious and satisfying curry dish.*

SERVES 4

100g/4oz dried chickpeas, soaked
   overnight in plenty of cold water
1 onion, sliced
1 clove garlic, crushed
4 tbsps oil
100g/4oz button mushrooms, wiped
   and sliced
1 tbsp garam masala
2 tbsps plain flour
½ tsp salt
Freshly ground black pepper
4 large chicken portions, skinned
140ml/¼ pint Heinz Tomato Ketchup
285ml/½ pint chicken stock

---

1. Drain and rinse chickpeas, then place them in a pan and cover with cold water and boil rapidly for 10 minutes.

2. Drain chickpeas and place in a large ovenproof dish.

3. Fry onion and garlic in half the oil for 3 minutes.

4. Add the mushrooms to the oil and cook for a further 5 minutes, then add to the chickpeas.

5. On a plate, mix together the garam masala, flour, salt and pepper.

6. Turn the chicken portions over in the spicy flour until well coated.

7. Heat the remaining oil in the pan and brown the chicken on both sides.

8. Place the browned chicken on top of the other ingredients in the ovenproof dish.

9. Mix Tomato Ketchup with stock and pour over the chicken.

10. Cover the dish and cook at 180°C/ 350°F/Gas Mark 4 for 1½ hours.

TIME: Preparation takes 35 minutes, cooking takes 1½ hours.

SERVING IDEA: Serve with rice and chutney.

SWEET AND SOUR PRAWNS

Like many Chinese stir-fry dishes, this is
nutritious and quick to prepare.

SERVES 4

Marinade
1 tbsp brandy
1 tbsp cornflour
1 egg, beaten

450g/1lb peeled prawns
2 tbsps white wine vinegar
2 tbsps sugar
3 tbsps Heinz Tomato Ketchup
1 tbsp soy sauce
1 tbsp cornflour
6 tbsps water
1 tsp sesame seed oil
½ tsp salt
5 tbsps plain flour
140ml/¼ pint oil
1 green pepper, deseeded and
  cut into chunks
1 bunch spring onions, trimmed and cut
  into 2.5cm/1in lengths

1. Mix the marinade ingredients, add the prawns and leave to marinate in a cool place for 15 minutes.

2. Mix the vinegar, sugar, ketchup, soy sauce, cornflour, water, sesame seed oil and salt in a small bowl.

3. Coat prawns in flour.

4. Heat oil in a large frying pan and fry prawns for 1 minute, remove with a slotted spoon and drain on kitchen paper.

5. Leave 1 tbsp oil in the pan and add the green pepper and spring onions and stir-fry for 2 minutes.

6. Add the Tomato Ketchup mixture and heat, stirring, until sauce thickens.

7. Add prawns, heat through and serve immediately.

TIME: Preparation and cooking takes about 25 minutes.

CHINESE STYLE LAMB

Try this for an unusual spicy Sunday lunch.

SERVES 6

140ml/¼ pint Heinz Tomato Ketchup
225ml/8fl.oz chicken or lamb stock
5 tbsps soy sauce
2 tsps ground 5 spice
2.5cm/1in piece ginger root, peeled and
 chopped
1 onion, chopped
1.25kg/2½ lb leg of lamb

---

1. Blend all ingredients except the lamb together in a large pan, bring to the boil, cover and simmer for 10 minutes.

2. Add lamb, cover and gently simmer for 1 hour turning over occasionally.

3. Leave to cool.

4. Skim off any fat that has solidified on the top of the stock, and take the leg of lamb out leaving the stock in the pan.

5. Place the lamb in a roasting tin and cook at 180°C/350°F/Gas Mark 4, basting occasionally with the stock, for 40 minutes or until juices run clear when the joint is pierced with a skewer.

6. While the joint is cooking, bring the stock in the pan to the boil, and boil until reduced by half to a sauce.

7. Sieve the sauce and serve with the lamb.

TIME: Preparation takes 2 hours, roasting takes 40 minutes.

SERVING IDEA: Serve with mangetout and baby sweetcorn.

VEGETABLE MASALA

This is a simple curry recipe to add spice to the supper table.

SERVES 4

1 onion, chopped
4 tbsps oil
1 tsp garam masala
1 tsp chilli powder
1 tsp ground turmeric
1 tsp black mustard seeds
1 tsp chopped ginger root
½ tsp salt
450g/1lb potatoes, peeled and diced
350g/12oz cauliflower, divided into
    small florets
6 tbsps Heinz Tomato Ketchup
225ml/8fl.oz water
100g/4oz peas
6 tbsps double cream

1. Fry onion in oil for 5 minutes.

2. Stir in spices and salt and gently fry for a further 5 minutes, stirring to prevent sticking.

3. Add potatoes, cauliflower, Tomato Ketchup and water, cover and simmer gently for 30 minutes.

4. Add peas and cook for a further 10 minutes.

5. Stir in cream, heat through and serve.

TIME: Preparation and cooking takes an hour.

Somerset Pies

*These lovely rustic pork and apple pies would make a
delicious and sustaining lunch or supper dish.*

SERVES 4

---

1 onion, sliced
2 tbsps oil
675g/1½ lbs shoulder or leg of pork, cut
   into 2.5cm/1in cubes
2 tbsps plain flour
Salt and freshly ground black pepper
285ml/½ pint chicken stock
1 x 128g can Heinz Apple Sauce
225g/8oz button mushrooms, wiped
   and sliced
2 tbsps fresh or 2 tsps dried chopped sage
225g/8oz plain flour
50g/2oz rolled oats
125g/5oz butter
4 tbsps water
1 tbsp milk

---

1. Fry onion in oil for 5 minutes.

2. Coat pork in flour seasoned with salt
and pepper.

3. Add pork to the onions and fry until
browned all over.

4. Remove from heat and stir in stock and
the Apple Sauce.

5. Return to heat, bring to the boil, cover
and simmer for 1 hour, stirring
occasionally.

6. Add mushrooms and sage, and cook for
a further 15 minutes.

7. Adjust seasoning and leave to cool.

8. Sift flour with a pinch of salt into a
bowl, and stir in the oats.

9. Rub the butter into the flour and oats
until the mixture resembles fine
breadcrumbs.

10. Make a well in the centre, add the
water and mix to give a soft dough.

11. Wrap and chill pastry for 20 minutes.

12. Divide cooled meat between 4
individual pie dishes.

13. Cut pastry in 4 and on a lightly floured
surface roll out each piece to overlap the
top of each pie dish by 2.5cm/1in.

14. Cut a strip of pastry from each and lay
along the rim of each dish.

15. Dampen pastry strip with water and
lay the main pastry on top, trimming off
any excess and pinching edges together to
seal.

16. Decorate pies using pastry trimmings,
and brush with milk.

17. Cook at 190°C/375°F/Gas Mark 5 for
25-30 minutes until pastry is golden.

TIME: Preparation takes 2 hours, baking takes 30 minutes.

CHICKEN AND PEACH PASSANDA

This fruity curry would be most refreshing on a summer's evening.

SERVES 4

3 tbsps oil
1 large onion, sliced
1 clove garlic, crushed
2 tsps garam masala
½ tsp turmeric
½ tsp chilli powder
2.5cm/1in piece of ginger root, peeled
   and finely chopped
1 bayleaf
1 stick cinnamon
Few black peppercorns
½ tsp salt
675g/1½ lbs chicken, skinned, boned
   and cut into 2.5/1in cubes
25g/1oz ground almonds
285ml/½ pint water
4 tbsps Heinz Mayonnaise
1 x 227g/8oz can sliced peaches, drained
   and roughly chopped

1. Heat oil in a large pan, and fry onion, garlic, spices, peppercorns and salt for 5 minutes.

2. Add chicken and ground almonds and fry for a further 5 minutes until chicken begins to brown.

3. Stir the water into the pan and simmer, uncovered, for 40 minutes, stirring occasionally.

4. Remove pan from heat and gradually stir in the Mayonnaise and peaches.

5. Return to heat and warm through.

TIME: Preparation and cooking takes about an hour.

SERVING IDEA: Serve with boiled rice and garnish with toasted flaked almonds.

LAMB AND LENTIL HOTPOT

*This elegant lamb dish makes a fine
centrepiece for the dinner table.*

SERVES 4

675g/1½ lbs best end of neck lamb
    stewing chops
1 tbsp plain flour
Salt and freshly ground black pepper
2 large onions, sliced
2 lambs kidneys, skinned, cored
    and sliced
675g/1½ lbs potatoes, peeled and sliced
Few sprigs fresh rosemary
1 x 435g can Heinz Lentil Soup

1. Coat chops in flour seasoned with salt
and pepper.

2. In a large ovenproof casserole dish,
layer chops, onions, kidneys, potatoes,
rosemary and seasoning.

3. Pour Lentil Soup over the top before
finishing with a layer of potatoes.

4. Cover with a tight-fitting lid and cook at
180°C/350°F/Gas Mark 4 for 2 hours.

5. Remove lid and cook for a further 30
minutes until potatoes are browned.

TIME: Preparation takes 5 minutes, cooking takes 2½ hours.

SERVING IDEA: Garnish with sprigs of rosemary.

Bean and Pork Casserole with Herb Scones

This wholesome recipe makes a very attractive dish on the dinner table.

SERVES 4

100g/4oz dried mixed beans, soaked overnight in plenty of cold water
450g/1lb belly of pork, cut into 2.5cm/1in cubes
2 tsps oil
5 cloves
100g/4oz button onions, peeled and halved
1 x 435g can Heinz Mulligatawny Soup
Juice of ½ lemon
140ml/¼ pint water
Salt and freshly ground black pepper

Herb scones
225g/8oz self-raising flour
40g/1½ oz butter
2 tsps dried mixed herbs
140ml/¼ pint milk

---

1. Drain and rinse the beans.

2. Place them in a pan, cover with cold water, bring to boil and boil rapidly for 10 minutes.

3. Turn down heat, cover and simmer for 30 minutes. Drain well.

4. Meanwhile, fry pork in oil in a pan until browned, then transfer to a casserole dish.

5. Stick the cloves into the onions and fry in the pan until onions have browned.

6. Add the onions to the pork in the casserole dish, and stir in the Mulligatawny Soup, the drained beans, lemon juice, water and seasoning to taste.

7. Cover with a tight-fitting lid and cook at 200°C/400°F/Gas Mark 6 for 1 hour.

8. For the scones, sift flour and a pinch of salt together into a bowl.

9. Quickly rub in the butter and stir in the herbs.

10. Make a well in the centre, add milk, reserving 1 tablespoon, and mix to form a soft dough.

11. Roll dough out on a lightly floured surface to 1cm/½ in thick.

12. Use a 5cm/2in fluted round pastry cutter, cut out 12 scones. Re-roll the trimmings to get 12 scones if necessary.

13. When the casserole has cooked for an hour, place the scones on top of the meat and cook uncovered for 15-20 minutes until scones are golden.

TIME: Preparation takes 20 minutes, cooking takes 1 hour 20 minutes.

SOUTHERN FRIED CHICKEN

This makes a delicious rich chicken dish.

SERVES 4

1.25kg/2½ lb chicken, cut into small
    joints and skinned
50g/2oz plain flour
2 tsps salt
Freshly ground black pepper
75g/3oz butter
6 tbsps oil
1 x 425g can Heinz Cream of Chicken
    Soup
140ml/¼ pint soured cream
1 tbsp cornflour

1. Coat the chicken in flour mixed with
salt and pepper to taste.

2. Fry chicken pieces in oil and butter
until browned on all sides.

3. Cover pan and cook on a low heat for
15 minutes or until chicken is cooked
through.

4. Remove chicken from pan and keep
hot.

5. Leave 1 tbsp of the cooking juices in
the pan and add the Cream of Chicken
Soup, reserving 2 tbsps, and the soured
cream. Gently heat through.

6. Mix cornflour with the reserved Cream
of Chicken Soup and stir into pan. Simmer
for 3 minutes. Serve sauce poured over
the chicken pieces.

TIME: Preparation takes 20 minutes.

COOK'S TIP: The chicken may need to be cooked in two batches if the pan is too small.

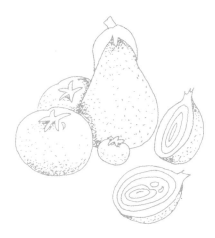

COWBOY HASH

*This is a substantial high-protein dish and would be well
complemented with a green leaf vegetable or salad.*

SERVES 8

1 medium onion, finely chopped
2 tbsps oil
675g/1½lbs beef mince
2 tbsps tomato purée
Salt
Freshly ground black pepper
275ml/½ pint beef stock
2 x 450g/15.9oz cans Heinz Baked Beans
  with 8 Pork Sausages
4 slices white bread, crusts removed
Oil
Chopped parsley

1. Fry the onion gently in the oil for 3 minutes.

2. Add the beef mince and fry until lightly coloured.

3. Add the tomato purée, salt and pepper to taste and the beef stock.

4. Simmer gently for 20-25 minutes until the meat is tender.

5. Add the Baked Beans and 8 Pork Sausages and heat through together.

6. Meanwhile, cut each slice of bread into triangles and fry in hot oil until lightly browned.

7. Garnish the prepared hash with the fried bread croûtons dipped into chopped parsley.

TIME: Preparation takes about 10 minutes, cooking takes about 35 minutes.

VARIATION: Add strips of red or green pepper, canned sweetcorn, or a few cooked peas.

BEAN AND SAUSAGE PIE

*This pie has an interesting blend of sweet and
savoury ingredients and is quick to prepare.*

SERVES 4-6

Pie Filling
1 x 450g/15.9oz can Heinz Baked Beans
    with 8 Pork Sausages
1 cooking apple, peeled and sliced
1 onion, peeled and sliced
1 green pepper, chopped
1 x 300g/10oz can button mushrooms,
    drained

225g/8oz wholemeal or shortcrust pastry
Beaten egg to glaze

---

1. Mix all the pie filling ingredients in a
pie dish.

2. Roll out the pastry to a size slightly
larger than the pie dish.

3. Wet the edge of the dish.

4. Cut a strip from the pastry and lay it on
to the edge of the dish.

5. Brush the pastry strip with water, then
lay the remaining pastry over the
ingredients in the dish, pressing it down
on to the pastry strip around the edge.

6. Knock up the edges of the pastry with a
knife.

7. Brush the top of the pie with beaten
egg and bake at 200°C/400°F/Gas Mark 6
for about 30 minutes until the top has
browned.

TIME: Preparation takes 15 minutes, cooking takes 30 minutes.

MULLIGATAWNY PIE

This curried beef pie is an original and
warming idea for a winter supper dish.

SERVES 4

225g/8oz wholemeal plain flour
Pch of salt
100g/4oz butter
2 tsps ground coriander
4 tbsps cold water
1 onion, chopped
1 tbsp oil
450g/1lb minced beef
1 x 435g can Heinz Mulligatawny Soup
1 dessert apple, peeled, cored
  and chopped
25g/1oz sultanas
Salt and freshly ground black pepper
1 tbsp milk
1 tsp cumin seeds

1. Sift the flour into a bowl and add a pinch of salt.

2. Rub the butter into the flour until it resembles fine breadcrumbs.

3. Stir in the ground coriander and make a well in the centre.

4. Add water to form a soft dough. Wrap and chill.

5. Meanwhile, gently fry the onion in oil for 3 minutes.

6. Add the minced beef and fry until browned.

7. Stir in the Mulligatawny Soup, apple, sultanas and seasoning to taste.

8. Cover and simmer for 45 minutes. Cool.

9. Divide pastry in half and roll out on a lightly floured surface.

10. Use half the pastry to line a 23cm/9in pie plate.

11. Spoon meat on top, dampen edges of pastry and cover with remaining pastry. Trim edges and pinch together to seal.

12. Brush with milk, garnish with pastry shapes, sprinkle with cumin seeds, and cook at 200°C/400°F/Gas Mark 6 for 30 minutes.

TIME: Preparation takes an hour and baking takes 30 minutes.

189

ONE POT BEEF

This is a rich and succulent beef dish.

SERVES 4

1.25kg/2½ lb joint rolled brisket of beef
15g/1/2oz butter
1 tbsp oil
1 clove garlic, crushed (optional)
225g/8oz button onions, peeled
450g/1lb new potatoes, scrubbed
225g/8oz baby carrots, washed
225g/8oz turnips, peeled and cut
　　into chunks
1 bayleaf
1 x 435g can Heinz Cream of
　　Tomato Soup
285ml/½ pint red wine
Salt and freshly ground black pepper

1. Fry beef in butter, oil and garlic in a large casserole dish, until browned on all sides. Remove beef from pot and put aside.

2. Add onions to pot and fry until browned.

3. Add rest of vegetables, bayleaf and the beef.

4. Pour the Cream of Tomato Soup and the red wine over the beef and season to taste.

5. Cover with a tight-fitting lid and cook at 170°C/325°F/Gas Mark 3 for 2½ hours or until beef is tender.

TIME: Preparation takes 15 minutes, cooking takes about 2½ hours.

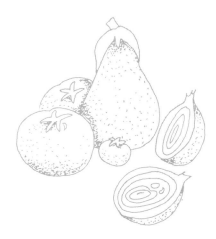

LAMB KLEFTICO

This Greek based recipe makes a stunning dinner party treat.

SERVES 6

2 onions, sliced
2 cloves garlic, crushed
1 bayleaf
1.8kg/4lb shoulder of lamb
1 x 435g can Heinz Cream of
 Tomato Soup
285ml/½ pint dry white wine
2 tsps dried or 2 tbsps fresh
 chopped oregano
450g/1lb tomatoes, skinned and quartered

1. Place onions, garlic, bayleaf and lamb in a large ovenproof dish.

2. Pour the soup and wine over the lamb, and sprinkle with oregano and season to taste.

3. Cover with a tight-fitting lid and cook at 180°C/350°F/Gas Mark 4 for 2½ hours turning lamb over occasionally.

4. Add tomatoes, and cook for a further 30 minutes.

5. Skim off fat before serving.

TIME: Preparation time is 5 minutes, cooking time is 3 hours.

COOK'S TIP: If you do not have a pan big enough for this dish, ask your butcher to cut the shoulder in half or buy two half shoulders instead.

SERVING IDEA: Serve garnished with sprigs of fresh oregano.

Marinated Mackerel

This mackerel recipe is full of flavour and character.

SERVES 4

4 mackerel, cleaned and heads removed
2 tbsps olive oil
1 tsp rubbed sage
Juice of ½ lemon
1 clove garlic, crushed
1 tsp chopped ginger root
Salt and freshly ground black pepper
4 rashers streaky bacon, rinds cut off
1 x 435g can Heinz Cream of
   Tomato Soup

1. Make three deep cuts on either side of each fish and place in an ovenproof dish.

2. Mix olive oil, sage, lemon juice, garlic, ginger and seasoning to taste together and pour over fish.

3. Cover and leave to marinate in a cool place for 1 hour.

4. Wrap each fish in a rasher of bacon and return to the marinade.

5. Pour the Cream of Tomato Soup over the fish, cover and bake at 190°C/375°F/Gas Mark 5 for 20 minutes.

6. Remove cover and cook for a further 15 minutes.

TIME: Preparation takes 10 minutes, marinading time is 1 hour,
baking takes about 40 minutes.

SERVING IDEA: Garnish with fresh sage.

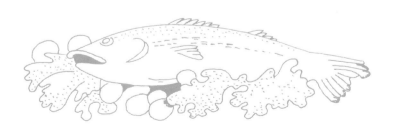

JAMBALAYA

This is a spicy savoury rice dish.

SERVES 4

225g/8oz white rice
225g/8oz chicken breast, skinned
  and diced
1 onion, chopped
1 clove garlic, crushed
15g/½ oz butter
1 tbsp oil
1 x 425g can Heinz Cream of
  Chicken Soup
Large pinch of ground cinnamon
½ tsp cayenne pepper
350g/12oz ham, diced
2 tomatoes, skinned, deseeded
  and chopped
1 tbsp fresh chopped parsley
Salt and freshly ground black pepper

1. Place rice in 225ml/8fl.oz water in a pan, cover and simmer for 10 minutes or until water has been absorbed.

2. Meanwhile, fry chicken, onion and garlic in butter and oil for 5 minutes.

3. Add rice, Cream of Chicken Soup, cinnamon and cayenne pepper, cover and simmer gently for 10 minutes, stirring occasionally.

4. Add ham, tomatoes, parsley and seasoning to taste, and cook for a further 5 minutes until rice is tender.

TIME: Cooking takes about 30 minutes.

SERVING IDEA: Garnish with parsley sprigs.

COD PROVENÇALE

*Cream of Tomato Soup gives this lovely fish dish a beautiful
colour and makes it very quick and easy to make.*

SERVES 4

1 onion, sliced
1 tbsp olive oil
1 green pepper, deseeded and sliced
1 yellow pepper, deseeded and sliced
4 cod steaks
1 x 435g can Heinz Cream of
   Tomato Soup
2 tsps dried mixed Herbes de Provence
Salt and freshly ground black pepper

1. Fry onion in the olive oil for 3 minutes.

2. Add green and yellow peppers, cover
and cook gently for 10 minutes.

3. Place in an ovenproof dish, and arrange
the cod steaks on top.

4. Pour the Cream of Tomato Soup over
the fish, sprinkle with herbs and season to
taste.

5. Cover and bake at 190°C/375°F/Gas
Mark 5 for 35-40 minutes.

TIME: Preparation takes 15 minutes, baking takes 35-40 minutes.

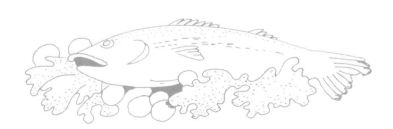

199

CHICKEN PAPRIKA

*A traditional Hungarian recipe, Chicken Paprika is a
delicious dish of tender strips of chicken in a tart, glistening sauce.*

SERVES 4

225g/8oz long-grain rice, rinsed
2 onions, sliced
1 tbsp oil
4 chicken breasts, skinned, boned and
    cut into strips
2 tsps paprika
4 tbsps Heinz All Seasons Herb &
    Garlic Dressing
1 tbsp lemon juice

1. Cook rice in a large pan of boiling
salted water for 18 minutes, drain and
rinse under hot water.

2. Meanwhile, fry the onions gently in the
oil for 4 minutes.

3. Add the chicken strips and stir-fry for 5
minutes.

4. Stir in the paprika and cook for a
further 2 minutes.

5. Blend in the Herb & Garlic Dressing
and lemon juice and heat through.

6. Serve with the boiled rice.

TIME: Preparation and cooking takes 20 minutes.

SERVING IDEA: Garnish with sprigs of parsley.

CREAMY POTATO PIE

*Serve this sizzling gratin as a vegetarian main dish with
salad, or as a vegetable dish to accompany meat or fish.*

SERVES 4

---

4 tbsps Heinz All Seasons Yogurt &
   Chive Dressing
Small pot of single cream
Salt and freshly ground black pepper
450g/1lb potatoes, peeled and
   thinly sliced
1 Spanish onion, sliced
50g/2oz cheese, grated

---

1. Mix Yogurt & Chive Dressing, cream
and seasoning together.

2. Arrange potato slices in layers in a
greased gratin dish, interleaving the layers
with the creamy mixture and onion slices.

3. Top with grated cheese and bake at
190°C/375°F/Gas Mark 4 for 25 minutes
until browned and sizzling.

SERVING IDEA: Serve garnished with fresh parsley sprigs.

LEEK AND BEAN HOTPOT

*This is a healthy high-fibre winter casserole,
good served with fresh green vegetables.*

SERVES 4

2 tsps oil
225g/8oz bacon or gammon, diced
225g/8oz carrots, chopped
225g/8oz leeks, sliced
1 x 450g/15.9oz can Heinz Baked Beans
450g/1lb potatoes, peeled and thinly
   sliced
15g/½ oz butter, melted

1. Heat the oil in a pan, add bacon or gammon and fry until browned.

2. Add the carrots and sizzle for a few minutes.

3. Add the leeks and Baked Beans and warm through.

4. Transfer half the mixture to an ovenproof dish, add a layer of half the potatoes, then the remaining bean mixture, and top with the rest of the sliced potatoes.

5. Sprinkle with melted butter and cover the dish with greaseproof paper. Bake at 200°C/400°F/Gas Mark 6 for about an hour or until the top is golden brown and the potatoes are tender.

TIME: Preparation takes 10 minutes, cooking time 1 hour.

TROUT FILLETS WITH HOT AND SOUR SAUCE

Trout makes a fine delicate dish and is readily available in supermarkets and fishmongers. You can fillet the fish yourself or buy it ready filleted.

SERVES 4

4 trout fillets (approximately 450g/1lb)
lemon juice

Sauce
150ml/5fl.oz single cream
4 tbsps Heinz Salad Cream
1 tbsp pickled gherkins, drained and
  chopped
1 tsp capers

1. Sprinkle the trout with lemon juice and poach in a little water in a large frying pan for 3-4 minutes. Keep them warm.

2. Heat the cream and Salad Cream very gently until quite hot, and stir in the gherkins and capers.

3. Serve each trout with a generous spoonful of sauce.

TIME: Preparation and cooking takes about 10 minutes.

SERVING IDEA: Serve with boiled new potatoes and a green salad.

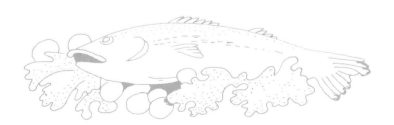

FISH AND BEAN PIE

*Add a little flair to the supper table with this
creative healthy recipe for all the family.*

SERVES 4

350g/12oz smoked haddock
150ml/¼ pint milk
1 small onion, finely chopped
25g/1oz butter
25g/1oz plain flour
225g/8oz can Heinz Italian Beans
1 tbsp chopped, fresh parsley
Grated rind of 1 lemon
Salt and freshly ground black pepper
1 egg, lightly beaten
2 x 225g/8oz packs frozen puff pastry,
　　defrosted

1. Place haddock and milk in a pan and simmer gently for 8 minutes or until fish flakes easily.

2. Strain milk into jug, flake fish discarding any skin and bones. Place in a long bowl.

3. Gently brown onion in butter for 3 minutes.

4. Stir in flour and cook for 1 minute over a low heat.

5. Remove from heat and gradually blend in milk, a little at a time.

6. Return to heat and bring to boil, stirring continuously. Simmer for 2 minutes until sauce thickens.

7. Stir fish, beans, parsley, lemon rind, seasoning and half beaten egg into sauce. Leave to cool.

8. Roll each pack of pastry into large rectangles, measuring about 30cm/12ins by 25cm/10ins on a lightly floured surface. Place one rectangle on top of the other.

9. Cut out a large fish shape, cutting through both thicknesses. Place one fish shape on to a large greased baking sheet.

10. Spoon filling on to pastry, leaving 1 cm/½ in pastry edge. Dampen edge with water, lightly roll remaining fish shape to 1cm/½ in bigger than other and place over filling, pinching edges to form a seal. Decorate fish with pastry trimmings, sealing with a little water.

11. Glaze with remaining beaten egg, and bake in a preheated oven at 200°C/400°F/ Gas Mark 6 for 25-30 minutes or until golden.

TIME: Preparation takes 30 minutes and baking takes 30 minutes.

SERVING IDEA: Garnish fish with fresh dill and lemon slices. Serve with salad.

RANCHERS' MEATLOAF

*This summertime treat is easy to prepare and can be
served both hot or cold as an accompaniment to a
barbecue or as a family main meal.*

SERVES 4-6

675g/1½ lbs minced beef
1 x 450g/15.9oz can Heinz Barbecue
   Beans
50g/2oz fresh white breadcrumbs
1 small onion, finely chopped
2 tsps chopped fresh herbs or ½ tsp dried
   mixed herbs
1 egg, beaten
Salt and freshly ground black pepper

1. Grease and base line a 900g/2lb loaf
tin.

2. Mix all the ingredients together with salt
and pepper to taste.

3. Pack into the loaf tin and bake for 1
hour at 180°C/350°F/Gas Mark 4 until
cooked through.

4. Cool for 15 minutes in the tin. Serve hot
or cold.

TIME: Preparation takes 5 minutes, cooking takes an hour plus 15 minutes resting time.

COOK'S TIP: Cover the tin with foil during cooking if the top seems cooked
but the inside still feels soft.

BARBECUE AND BACON FLAN

*This makes an interesting change from
the usual egg-based flans.*

SERVES 6

225g/8oz shortcrust pastry
Beaten egg
1 onion, thinly sliced
1 tbsp oil
3 rashers lean bacon, cut into strips
1 tsp chopped fresh thyme or a pinch of
    dried thyme
2 x 450g/15.9oz cans Heinz Barbecue
    Beans
Salt and freshly ground pepper
150g/5oz Cheddar or Edam cheese,
    thinly sliced

1. Roll out the pastry fairly thinly and line a 23cm/9in loose-bottomed fluted flan tin, pressing up the edges well.

2. Line the pastry with greaseproof paper and baking beans, pasta or rice, and bake at 190°C/375°F/Gas Mark 5 for 15 minutes.

3. Remove the paper and beans, pasta or rice, brush the pastry with the beaten egg and return to the oven for a further 10 minutes.

4. Meanwhile, fry the onion in the oil for 3 minutes, add the bacon and fry for a further 4 minutes.

5. Stir in the thyme, Barbecue Beans, and salt and pepper to taste, and heat through.

6. Spoon the mixture into the pastry case and top with the thinly sliced cheese. Return to the oven for about 8 minutes until the cheese starts to melt. Serve piping hot.

TIME: Cooking takes 45 minutes.

SERVING IDEA: Serve garnished with fresh thyme and accompanied by a leafy salad.

CHICKEN WITH SWEET AND SOUR BEAN SAUCE

*This is an attractive festive dish that would be
particularly welcome in the winter months.*

SERVES 6

1 large onion, thinly sliced
6 tbsps oil
1 green pepper, deseeded and cut into
    thin strips
1 red pepper, deseeded and cut into
    thin strips
1 clove garlic, finely chopped
Pinch of ground ginger
Salt and freshly ground black pepper
3 tbsps red wine vinegar
2 tbsps brown sugar
275ml/½ pint apple juice
275ml/½ pint fresh unsweetened
    orange juice
2 tbsps cornflour
1 large carrot, peeled and coarsely grated
2 rings pineapple, finely chopped
6 even-sized chicken joints
2 x 450g/15.9oz cans Heinz Barbecue
    Beans

1. Heat half the oil in a large deep pan
and fry the chicken joints evenly until
golden on all sides.

2. Meanwhile, fry the onion gently in the
remaining oil for 3 minutes.

3. Add the pepper strips and garlic and fry
for a further 2-3 minutes.

4. Add the ginger, salt and pepper to taste,
red wine vinegar, brown sugar and fruit
juices, bring to the boil and simmer gently
for 10 minutes.

5. Blend the cornflour to a paste with 4
tbsps cold water, blend in a little of the
hot liquid and then return to the pan, stir
over the heat until the sauce has
thickened.

6. Add the carrot and pineapple to the
sauce and simmer for 10 minutes.

7. Stir in the Barbecue Beans, heat
through, and serve poured over the fried
chicken.

TIME: Cooking takes about ½ hour.

VARIATIONS: Brown the chicken in a deep pan, then add the prepared sauce without the
Barbecue Beans, simmer covered for 25 minutes, then add the Beans and heat through.

COOK'S TIP: For a really festive flavour, add a little rum to the sauce.

LAMB WITH BARBECUE BEAN SAUCE

Barbecue Beans lend themselves perfectly to this rich, sweet lamb recipe.

SERVES 4

4 large or 8 small lamb chops
Oil
Salt and freshly ground black pepper
275ml/½ pint red wine
1 bayleaf
Grated rind of 1 lemon
1 clove garlic, crushed
3 tbsps cider vinegar
3 tbsps brown sugar
1 x 450g/15.9oz can Heinz Barbecue Beans
12 canned peach slices
2 spring onions, chopped (optional)

1. Put the lamb chops into a shallow dish.

2. Mix 4 tbsps oil with salt and pepper to taste, red wine, bayleaf, lemon rind and garlic, and spoon over the lamb.

3. Cover and chill for 3-4 hours.

4. Drain off the marinade from the lamb, putting the lamb to one side and the marinade in a pan.

5. Add the vinegar to the marinade in the pan and bubble fairly briskly until reduced by about one third.

6. Add the sugar and Barbecue Beans to the sauce and 6 of the peach slices, roughly chopped, mix together and keep warm on one side of the barbecue.

7. Brush the lamb chops on both sides with a little oil and place on the grill of the preheated barbecue. Cook for 6-7 minutes on each side.

8. Arrange the cooked chops on a serving dish, spoon the Barbecue Bean sauce over and around the chops, and top each chop with thin slivers of peach (cut each peach slice into three) and chopped spring onion.

TIME: The lamb chops are left to marinade for 3-4 hours, preparation time thereafter is about 15-20 minutes.

SERVING IDEA: Garnish with parsley or watercress.

Barbecued Lamb with Apricots

*Barbecue Beans, ginger and apricots give an
outdoor smoky flavour to an easy indoor dish.*

SERVES 4

100g/4oz dried apricots, soaked in cold
   water overnight
1 large onion, thinly sliced
3 tbsps oil
¼ tsp ground ginger
8 small trimmed lamb cutlets
1 x 450g/15.9oz can Heinz Barbecue
   Beans
½ cucumber, deseeded and cut into thick
   strips
Salt and freshly ground black pepper

1. Grill the cutlets gently, browning them
evenly.

2. Meanwhile, fry the sliced onion in the
oil for 3 minutes.

3. Stir in the ginger and add the Barbecue
Beans, apricots and seasoning to taste.
Simmer gently for 5 minutes.

4. Add the strips of cucumber, heat
through and serve spooned over the
grilled cutlets.

TIME: Cooking takes 20-25 minutes.

SERVING IDEA: Serve with baked jacket potatoes.

COOK'S TIP: The cutlets should be tender, but still slightly pink in the centre.

VARIATION: The cutlets can be fried until tender in the pan, after frying the onion, and
then stirred together with the other ingredients.

Spiced Chicken Casserole

This would make a delicious and unusual supper party dish.

SERVES 4

25g/1oz butter
1 tbsp oil
4 chicken joints, wiped
2 onions, quartered
1 red pepper, deseeded and cut
   into chunks
1 green pepper, deseeded and cut
   into chunks
100g/4oz garlic sausage, roughly chopped
1 bayleaf
grated rind and juice of ½ lemon
425ml/¾ pint chicken stock
Salt and freshly ground black pepper
1 x 450g/15.9oz can Heinz Curried Beans
2 tsps cornflour (optional)
4 tbsps natural yogurt

Garnish
12 triangles fried bread
Lemon slices

1. Brown chicken on all sides in the butter and oil in a large frying pan, and lift out, shaking off the fat, and transfer into a large casserole dish.

2. Gently fry the onions in the frying pan for 5 minutes and spoon these into the casserole, with all the cooking juices.

3. Add peppers, sausage, bayleaf, lemon rind and juice, stock, and salt and pepper to taste, and mix well together.

4. Cover the casserole and cook in oven at 180°C/350°F/Gas Mark 4 for 1 hour.

5. Stir in the Curried Beans, and add the cornflour mixed with a little water if a thicker sauce is preferred. Return the casserole to the oven for a further 30 minutes.

6. Adjust seasoning to taste and serve drizzled with yogurt and garnished with the fried bread triangles and lemon slices.

TIME: Preparation takes 10 minutes, cooking takes 1½ hours.

221

WINTER PORK AND BEAN HOTPOT

This is a nourishing recipe to keep out the winter chill.

SERVES 4

2 tbsps oil
100g/4oz onion, chopped
450g/1lb shoulder pork, cubed
225g/8oz carrots, peeled and thickly sliced
½ chicken stock cube
150ml/¼ pint water
2 x 225g/7.94oz cans Heinz Curried Beans
Worcestershire sauce
Salt
Chopped parsley

1. Fry onion in oil until transparent.

2. Add pork and brown well.

3. Stir in carrots, stock cube and water, bring to boil, cover and simmer for 1 hour.

4. Stir in Curried Beans and season to taste with Worcestershire sauce and salt.

5. Heat through and serve sprinkled with the chopped parsley.

TIME: Cooking takes about 1½ hours.

SHEPHERD'S SURPRISE

*This tangy shepherd's pie is quick to assemble and
can be prepared well in advance of baking.*

SERVES 4

1 onion, chopped
2 tbsps oil
1 clove garlic, finely chopped
350g/12oz minced lamb
1 tbsp tomato purée
1 tbsp Worcestershire sauce
4 tbsps grated Parmesan cheese
Salt and freshly ground black pepper
2 x 225g/7.94oz cans Heinz Curried Beans
450g/1lb potatoes, peeled cooked and
    mashed
2 egg yolks
15g/½ oz butter
½ tsp French mustard

1. Fry the onion gently in the oil for 3 minutes.

2. Add the garlic and lamb and fry until evenly coloured.

3. Drain off and discard any excess fat from the meat.

4. Stir the tomato purée, Worcestershire sauce, half the grated Parmesan cheese, salt and pepper to taste, and the Curried Beans into the meat, and mix well.

5. Spoon mixture into a greased ovenproof dish.

6. Beat the potato with the egg yolks, butter, mustard and salt and pepper to taste.

7. Fork the potato over the meat pie filling, and sprinkle with the remaining grated cheese.

8. Bake at 190°C/375°F/Gas Mark 5 for 35-40 minutes and serve piping hot.

TIME: Preparation takes 25 minutes and baking takes 35-40 minutes.

SERVING IDEA: Serve with a cucumber and yogurt salad.

Bean Moussaka

*Baked Beans are not a traditional moussaka ingredient,
but the meat, Baked Beans, cheese and yogurt blend is irresistible,
and the addition of Baked Beans also makes the dish more
economical as less meat is required.*

SERVES 4-6

1 large onion, chopped
3 tbsps olive oil
1 large clove garlic, crushed
350g/12oz minced lean lamb
2 tbsps tomato purée
1 tsp dried oregano
2 x 450g/15.9oz cans Heinz Baked Beans
Salt and freshly ground black pepper
3 large potatoes, peeled and thinly sliced
100g/4oz grated or crumbled Feta cheese
150ml/¼ pint soured cream
150ml/¼ pint natural yogurt
2 eggs

1. Fry the chopped onion gently in the oil for 3-4 minutes.

2. Add the garlic and minced lamb and fry until the meat is evenly browned.

3. Stir in the tomato purée, oregano, Baked Beans and salt and pepper to taste, and simmer for 5 minutes.

4. Spoon half of the meat and Baked Bean mixture into a deep, greased ovenproof dish, cover with a little crumbled cheese and half the sliced potato.

5. Add another layer of meat mixture, a little more crumbled cheese and the remaining sliced potato.

6. Beat the soured cream and yogurt with the eggs and spread over the top of the potato, and sprinkle with the remaining cheese.

7. Bake at 190°C/375°F/Gas Mark 5 for 45-50 minutes until it is nicely browned and the potatoes are tender.

TIME: Preparation takes 20 minutes, cooking time 45-50 minutes.

VARIATION: Feta cheese is the traditional Greek cheese to use in moussaka and can be bought from most large supermarkets, but Cheddar can be used as an alternative.

BEAN AND PRAWN CHOW MEIN

*Dried beans are a traditional ingredient of Chinese cooking.
Here, Heinz Curried Beans are used to make a
spicy and speedy noodle dish.*

SERVES 4

1 onion, finely chopped
2 tbsps oil
1 clove garlic, crushed
2 sticks celery, finely chopped
1 green pepper, deseeded and finely
  chopped
2 x 225g/7.94oz cans Heinz Curried Beans
150ml/¼ pint chicken stock
4 canned water chestnuts, thinly sliced
½ tsp grated fresh root ginger
225g/8oz peeled prawns
2 tbsps chopped parsley
350g/12oz yellow or green noodles
Salt and freshly ground black pepper
Melted butter or oil

1. Fry the chopped onion gently in the oil
for 3 minutes.

2. Add the garlic and celery and fry for a
further 3 minutes.

3. Add the green pepper, Curried Beans,
chicken stock, water chestnuts and root
ginger and simmer gently for a bare 5
minutes.

4. Stir the prawns and parsley into the
sauce and leave to stand off the heat.
(This gives the flavours in the sauce a
chance to mingle without the risk of over-
cooking the ingredients.)

5. Cook the noodles in a large pan of
boiling salted water until just tender, drain
thoroughly and toss in melted butter or
oil.

6. Heat the prawn and bean sauce
through gently, pile the hot noodles on to
a serving dish and top with the sauce, or
serve in separate dishes.

TIME: Preparation of the sauce takes 15 minutes and the noodles
cook in about 10 minutes.

COOK'S TIP: Be careful not to overcook the vegetables, they should
keep their crunchy texture.

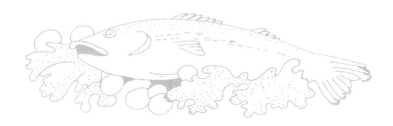

HAM, BEAN AND SAUSAGE CASSEROLE

This hearty dish combines the old favourites pork and beans with pasta.

SERVES 4

1 onion, finely chopped
2 tbsps oil
1 clove garlic, crushed
8 medium-sized sausages
75g/3oz ham in one thick slice, cut into cubes
2 x 450g/15.9oz cans Heinz Baked Beans
Salt and freshly ground black pepper
1 tbsp chopped fresh thyme
150ml/¼ pint chicken stock
75g/3oz pasta shells

1. Fry the chopped onion gently in the oil for 3 minutes.

2. Add the garlic and sausages and fry until evenly browned on all sides.

3. Stir in the ham, Baked Beans, salt and pepper to taste, thyme and chicken stock and bring to the boil.

4. Stir in the pasta shells and transfer the mixture to a casserole dish.

5. Cover and cook at 180°C/350°F/Gas Mark 4 for about 40 minutes until the pasta shells are cooked.

6. Serve piping hot with a green leaf vegetable.

COOK'S TIP: During cooking check that the casserole is not becoming too dry, and if necessary add a little extra chicken stock.

Beef and Broad Bean Casserole with Poppy Seed Dumplings

This lovely, old-fashioned, wholesome dish would be comforting on a cold autumn night.

SERVES 4

675g/1½ lbs stewing steak, cubed
1 tbsp oil
1 large onion, sliced
1 x 435g can Heinz Lentil Soup
Salt and freshly ground black pepper
450g/1lb fresh broad beans or 225g/8oz
   frozen shelled broad beans

Dumplings
225g/8oz self-raising flour
Pinch of salt
100g/4oz shredded suet
1 tbsp poppy seeds
140ml/¼ pint cold water

1. Fry the stewing steak in the oil over a high heat until browned on all sides, then transfer it to a large ovenproof dish.

2. Add onion, Lentil Soup and seasoning to taste.

3. Cover and cook at 180°C/350°F/Gas Mark 4 for 1 hour.

4. Shell the broad beans if necessary, add to casserole and cook for a further 30 minutes.

5. Meanwhile, for the dumplings, sift the flour and salt into a large bowl.

6. Stir in the suet and poppy seeds.

7. Make a well in the centre, add water and stir with a knife to form a soft dough.

8. Divide dough into 8 rounds, place in the casserole, cover and cook for a further 20 minutes or until dumplings have risen.

TIME: Preparation takes 10 minutes, cooking takes about 2 hours.

COURGETTE AND LENTIL LOAF

This is an easy and delicious vegetarian loaf,
equally good eaten hot or cold.

SERVES 4

350g/12oz courgettes, wiped
1 x 435g can Heinz Lentil Soup
1 small onion, grated
100g/4oz fresh white breadcrumbs
25g/1oz chopped mixed nuts
3 eggs, beaten
1 tsp grated nutmeg
Salt and freshly ground black pepper

1. Grease a 900g/2lb loaf tin and line with greaseproof paper.

2. Slice 1 courgette and arrange the slices to cover the base of the loaf tin.

3. Grate the remaining courgettes and place in a large mixing bowl.

4. Add the rest of the ingredients to the courgettes and mix well.

5. Pour mixture into the loaf tin and cook at 190°C/375°F/Gas Mark 5 for 1 hour.

6. Leave to rest for 5 minutes before turning out.

7. Serve hot or cold, sliced.

TIME: Preparation takes 5 minutes, cooking takes an hour.

Mushroom and Cream Cheese Quiche

This is a rich, creamy quiche, best served with a plain green salad.

SERVES 6

Pastry
150g/6oz plain flour
75g/3oz butter
Pinch of salt

2 tbsps sesame seeds
3 tbsps cold water
150g/6oz button mushrooms, wiped and sliced
15g/½ oz butter
1 x 425g can Heinz Cream of Mushroom Soup
100g/4oz cream cheese
3 eggs, beaten
Salt and freshly ground black pepper

1. Sift flour and salt into a bowl.

2. Rub in the butter until it resembles fine breadcrumbs.

3. Stir in sesame seeds.

4. Make a well in the centre, add the water and mix to form a soft dough.

5. Wrap pastry and chill for 20 minutes.

6. Roll out pastry on a lightly floured surface, and use to line a greased 20cm/8in quiche dish.

7. Bake blind, lined with greaseproof paper and baking beans, at 200°C/400°F/Gas Mark 6 for 15 minutes. Leave to cool.

8. Fry mushrooms in butter for 5 minutes, and leave to cool.

9. Blend Cream of Mushroom Soup, cream cheese and eggs together, and season to taste.

10. Add the mushrooms to the mixture and pour into the pastry case.

11. Cook at 190°C/375°F/Gas Mark 5 for 35-40 minutes until set and beginning to brown.

TIME: Preparation takes 50 minutes, cooking takes 35-40 minutes.

SERVING IDEA: Serve hot or cold, garnished with a sprig of parsley.

CANNELLONI WITH ASPARAGUS SAUCE

*These delicate Italian pasta rolls can be
served as a starter or main course.*

SERVES 4 AS A MAIN COURSE, OR 6 AS A STARTER

1 small onion, chopped
1 clove garlic, crushed
15g/½ oz butter
225g/8oz button mushrooms, wiped and
　chopped
1 x 230g/8.1oz can chopped tomatoes
1 tbsp chopped fresh basil
Salt and freshly ground black pepper
12 tubes cannelloni
1 x 425g can Heinz Cream of
　Asparagus Soup
50g/2oz Cheddar cheese, grated

1. Gently fry the onion and garlic in butter
for 3 minutes.

2. Add the mushrooms and fry until any
liquid produced has evaporated.

3. Remove pan from heat, stir in the
tomatoes, basil and seasoning to taste.

4. Using a teaspoon fill each tube with the
mushroom stuffing.

5. Lay the stuffed cannelloni tubes in an
ovenproof dish, pour the Cream of
Asparagus Soup over them, sprinkle with
cheese and cook at 200°C/400°F/Gas Mark
6 for 30 minutes.

TIME: Preparation time is 20 minutes, cooking time is 30 minutes.

SERVING IDEA: Serve garnished with sprigs of fresh basil.

CHICKEN WITH MUSHROOM AND TARRAGON

*This delicate creamy sauce transforms a chicken
joint into a fine and special dish.*

SERVES 4

15g/½ oz plain flour
Salt and freshly ground black pepper
4 chicken breasts, skinned
1 tbsp oil
225g/8oz button mushrooms, wiped
   and sliced
140ml/¼ pint dry white wine
1 x 425g can Heinz Cream of
   Mushroom Soup
1 tbsp fresh chopped or 1 tsp dried
   tarragon

1. Season flour with salt and pepper to taste and coat the chicken breasts.

2. Heat oil in a large frying pan and fry chicken until browned all over, then transfer them to an ovenproof dish.

3. Add mushrooms to pan and fry for 5 minutes.

4. Add wine and boil until liquid has reduced by half.

5. Stir in Cream of Mushroom Soup and tarragon, heat through, season to taste and pour over the chicken.

6. Cover the dish and cook at 200°C/400°F/Gas Mark 6 for 30 minutes.

TIME: Preparation takes 20-25 minutes, cooking takes 30 minutes.

SERVING IDEA: Serve garnished with sprigs of fresh tarragon and accompanied by young fresh vegetables.

Prawn Stuffed Plaice with Peppers

These appetizing rolls of fish swimming in their creamy asparagus sauce
are delicious served with boiled new potatoes.

SERVES 4

100g/4oz peeled prawns
4 small plaice, filleted and skinned
Salt and freshly ground black pepper
½ yellow pepper, deseeded and cut
   into strips
1 pimento, thinly sliced
1 x 425g can Heinz Cream of
   Asparagus Soup

1. Divide prawns equally between plaice fillets, laying them on the fish, and season with salt and pepper.

2. Roll up each fillet with prawns inside and place in an ovenproof dish.

3. Blanch yellow pepper in boiling water for 2 minutes and drain.

4. Decorate the stuffed fillets with strips of pepper and slices of pimento.

5. Carefully pour the Cream of Asparagus Soup over the fish, without dislodging the peppers.

6. Cook at 190°C/375°F/Gas Mark 5 for 30 minutes, and serve.

TIME: Preparation takes 5 minutes, cooking takes 30 minutes.

242

ITALIAN TUNA BAKE

*This is a quick and useful dish which could be
prepared well in advance of baking.*

SERVES 4

150g/6oz green tagliatelle
Salt
1 red pepper, deseeded and chopped
2 courgettes, sliced
25g/1oz butter
1 x 198g/7oz can tuna in brine, drained
1 x 425g can Heinz Cream of
    Mushroom Soup
25g/1oz fresh white breadcrumbs
1 tbsp grated Parmesan cheese

1. Cook tagliatelle in plenty of boiling salted water for 8 minutes or according to packet instructions.

2. Drain the pasta and place in a large buttered ovenproof dish.

3. Fry pepper and courgettes in butter for 5 minutes, then spoon over the pasta.

4. Spread the tuna out over the vegetables.

5. Pour the Cream of Mushroom Soup over the tuna.

6. Mix the breadcrumbs and cheese together and sprinkle over the top of the dish.

7. Cook at 200°C/400°F/Gas Mark 6 for 30 minutes.

TIME: Preparation takes 15 minutes, cooking takes 30 minutes.

SERVING IDEA: Garnish with a sprig of oregano.

SAUSAGE GOUGÈRE

This succulent dish is a rather superior cousin of toad-in-the-hole.

SERVES 4

50g/2oz butter
140ml/¼ pint water
65g/2½ oz plain flour, sifted
Pinch of salt
2 eggs, beaten
450g/1lb sausages
2 tsps wholegrain mustard
8 slices rindless streaky bacon
1 x 425g can Heinz Cream of Celery Soup
Freshly ground black pepper
25g/1oz fresh white breadcrumbs

---

1. For the choux pastry, melt the butter in water and bring to the boil.

2. Remove from the heat and add flour all at once, then beat with a wooden spoon until a smooth paste is formed which leaves the sides of the pan clean.

3. Allow to cool for several minutes.

4. Add salt to the eggs, and beat this into the paste a little at a time as vigorously as possible to give a glossy mixture and piping consistency.

5. Allow this mixture to cool completely.

6. Put mixture in a piping bag fitted with a large plain vegetable nozzle.

7. Prick sausages all over with a fork.

8. Coat sausages in mustard and wrap each in a rasher of bacon, then place them in an ovenproof dish.

9. Cook at 200°C/400°F/Gas Mark 6 for 20 minutes.

10. Pour Cream of Celery Soup over the bacon-wrapped sausages, and season with pepper.

11. Pipe choux pastry around the edge of the dish, and sprinkle the breadcrumbs over the sausages.

12. Cook for 40 minutes until pastry is well risen and cooked through.

TIME: Preparation takes 20 minutes, cooking takes 1 hour.

COOK'S TIP: You may not need to add all the beaten egg to the paste.

SERVING IDEA: Garnish with a sprig of parsley.

BAKED FENNEL WITH BLUE CHEESE

*This Italian-based fennel bake, bathed in tomato and
wine goes beautifully with roast meats.*

SERVES 4

450g/1lb fennel, trimmed and thinly sliced
1 small onion, thinly sliced
140ml/¼ pint Heinz Tomato Ketchup
140ml/¼ pint dry white wine
Salt and freshly ground black pepper
50g/2oz Danish blue cheese, crumbled
50g/2oz fresh white breadcrumbs

1. Place fennel and onion in an ovenproof
dish.

2. Blend Tomato Ketchup, wine and
seasoning to taste, and pour over the
fennel.

3. Cover and cook at 180°C/350°F/Gas
Mark 4 for 1 hour.

4. Sprinkle cheese and breadcrumbs over
fennel, and cook, uncovered, for a further
20 minutes.

TIME: Preparation takes 5-10 minutes, cooking takes 1 hour 20 minutes.

SERVING IDEA: Garnish with tomato slices and watercress.

VEGETABLE CROQUETTES

*This recipe is an excellent way of
revitalising left-over vegetables.*

SERVES 4

675g/1½ lbs cooked potato and
   vegetables
6 tbsps Heinz Tomato Ketchup
Salt and freshly ground black pepper
25g/1oz plain flour
1 large egg, beaten
150g/6oz fresh white breadcrumbs
Oil for frying

---

1. Roughly mash vegetables and mix with
Tomato Ketchup and salt and pepper to
taste.

2. Divide into 16 equal portions and form
each into sausage-shaped croquettes.

3. Roll each croquette in flour, egg, then
breadcrumbs to coat.

4. Heat oil in a large frying pan and
shallow fry the croquettes in batches until
golden all over.

5. Drain the croquettes on kitchen paper
before serving.

TIME: Preparation and cooking takes 30-45 minutes.

SERVING IDEA: Garnish with watercress.

VEGETABLE FRITTERS WITH A TOMATO DIPPING SAUCE

These make good party 'eats' to accompany drinks.

SERVES 4

Batter
100g/4oz plain flour
1½ tsps baking powder
½ tsp salt
2 eggs, beaten
140ml/¼ pint milk

Dipping sauce
6 tbsps Heinz Tomato Ketchup
1 tbsp mushroom ketchup
1 tbsp soft brown sugar
½ small onion, finely chopped
Juice and grated rind of ½ lemon

350g/12oz cooked vegetables, sliced or
    chopped into bite-size pieces
Oil for frying

1. For the batter, sift flour, baking powder and salt into a bowl.

2. Beat the eggs with the milk.

3. Make a well in the centre of the flour, pour in the eggs and milk, and beat to a smooth batter.

4. Leave the batter mixture to stand in a cool place for at least 1 hour.

5. For the dip, combine the dipping sauce ingredients in a small pan, bring to the boil, and simmer gently for 5 minutes.

6. Add vegetables to the batter.

7. Heat .5cm/¼ in oil in a frying pan.

8. Drop pieces of batter-coated vegetable into the hot oil and fry on both sides until golden and crisp.

9. Drain the fritters on kitchen paper and serve hot with the sauce.

TIME: Preparation takes about 1 hour 15 minutes, cooking takes 20 minutes.

RED CABBAGE WITH APPLES

*This warm vegetable dish would be excellent with
pork or as part of a vegetarian meal.*

SERVES 4

1 small onion, chopped
1 tbsp oil
450g/1lb red cabbage, shredded
1 dessert apple, peeled, cored and
 chopped
225g/8oz potatoes, peeled and diced
25g/1oz sultanas
1 x 435g can Heinz Lentil Soup
Salt and freshly ground black pepper
1 tbsp chopped fresh mixed herbs

1. Fry the onion gently in the oil for 5
minutes in a large pan.

2. Add the red cabbage, apple, potatoes,
sultanas, Lentil Soup and seasoning to
taste.

3. Cover and simmer for 20 minutes or
until vegetables are tender.

4. Stir the herbs and serve.

TIME: Preparation takes 5 minutes, cooking takes 25 minutes.

CRUNCHY COLESLAW

This is a refreshing, light coleslaw.

SERVES 4

4 tbsps Weight Watchers from Heinz
    Reduced Calorie Dressing
4 tbsps low-fat natural yogurt
Squeeze of lemon juice
½ tsp paprika
Salt
180g/6oz white cabbage, shredded
90g/3oz carrots, shredded or
    coarsely grated
90g/3oz celery, finely chopped
1 medium apple, peeled, cored
    and chopped
1 onion, finely sliced
3 tbsps chopped parsley

1. Mix the Reduced Calorie dressing with the yogurt and season with lemon juice, paprika and salt to taste.

2. Stir in the chopped and shredded vegetables and apple and transfer to a serving bowl.

3. Garnish with sliced onion and chopped parsley.

TIME: Preparation takes 10 minutes.

CALORIES: 69 per serving.

SEAFOOD SAUCE

*This delicious low-calorie salmon-pink sauce can be rustled
up rapidly and raises the tone of a seafood supper.*

SERVES 4

---

4 tbsps Weight Watchers from Heinz
    Reduced Calorie Dressing
4 tbsps low-fat natural yogurt
8 tsps tomato ketchup
8 tsps lemon juice
2-3 drops Tabasco

1. Mix the Reduced Calorie Dressing,
yogurt, ketchup and lemon juice.

2. Add Tabasco to taste, being careful not
to add too much.

TIME: Preparation takes 2 minutes.

CALORIES: 43 per serving.

SERVING IDEA: Garnish with cucumber and serve with shellfish
or cold cooked white fish.

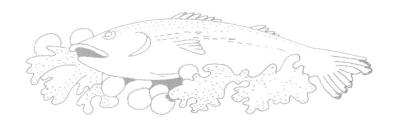

CURRIED RATATOUILLE

*The mulligatawny soup added to this classic Mediterranean
dish gives it a lovely savoury richness.*

SERVES 4

1 aubergine, halved and sliced
1 onion, sliced
2 tbsps oil
½ red pepper, deseeded and cut
  into chunks
½ green pepper, deseeded and cut
  into chunks
1 large courgette, sliced
4 tomatoes, skinned and quartered
1 x 435g can Heinz Mulligatawny Soup
Salt and freshly ground black pepper
2 tbsps fresh chopped coriander

1. Place aubergine in a colander and sprinkle with 1 tablespoon of salt. Leave to stand for 30 minutes to allow bitter juices to drain out.

2. Wash aubergine thoroughly and dry well.

3. Fry onion and aubergine in oil for 5 minutes over a gentle heat.

4. Add peppers and courgette and fry for a further 5 minutes.

5. Add tomatoes, Mulligatawny Soup and season to taste.

6. Cover and simmer for 10 minutes until vegetables are tender.

7. Stir in the fresh coriander just before serving.

TIME: Preparation takes 35 minutes, cooking takes about 20 minutes.

260

CUCUMBER BOATS

This makes attractive party finger food.

SERVES 4-6

1 cucumber
1 x 210g can Heinz Pasta Salad
½ red pepper, cut in thin strips
Few sprigs fresh dill

1. Slice the cucumber in half.

2. Cut into 5cm/2in sections, remove the seeds, and scoop out the flesh into a mixing bowl.

3. Mix the cucumber flesh with the Pasta Salad.

4. Spoon the mixture into the cucumber boats.

5. Decorate with thin strips of red pepper and sprigs of fresh dill.

TIME: Preparation takes 5 minutes.

BEAN AND NUT STUFFING

This unusual fruity stuffing will enliven any bird.

SUFFICIENT FOR A MEDIUM-SIZED TURKEY

50g/2oz butter
100g/4oz blanched almonds, roughly chopped
1 medium onion, finely chopped
1 clove garlic, crushed
Salt and freshly ground black pepper
175g/6oz fresh wholemeal breadcrumbs
1-2 eggs beaten
75g/3oz dried apricots, chopped
75g/3oz pitted prunes, chopped
75g/3oz sultanas
Grated rind and juice ½ orange
1 x 450g/15.9oz can Heinz Baked Beans
1 cooking apple, grated

1. Heat the butter in a pan and fry the nuts until lightly golden.

2. Add the onion and garlic and fry for a further 3 minutes.

3. Add salt and pepper to taste.

4. Put breadcrumbs in a bowl, add the fried nuts and onion, a little of the beaten egg and the remaining ingredients. Mix, adding extra egg if too stiff.

5. Spoon the mixture into bird.

TIME: Preparation 10 minutes.

TARRAGON SAUCE

*This delicious warm herby sauce can even
be enjoyed by the weight watcher.*

SERVES 4

30g/1oz butter or margarine
4 tsps Weight Watchers from Heinz
   Reduced Calorie Dressing
2 tsps white wine vinegar
2 tsps finely chopped onion
1 tsp chopped parsley
½ tsp dried tarragon

1. Heat butter or margarine gently in a small saucepan.

2. Add the Reduced Calorie Dressing and the wine vinegar and stir together for 2-3 minutes over very low heat.

3. Add remaining ingredients and stir for a further 2-3 minutes.

4. Serve warm.

TIME: Preparation and cooking takes 10 minutes.

CALORIES: 63 per serving.

SERVING IDEA: Serve spooned on to grilled steak or fish.

FRUITY CURRY SAUCE

This low-calorie hot and sweet sauce makes an unusual
change and is made from storecupboard ingredients.

SERVES 4

2 onions, chopped
4 cloves garlic, crushed
1 tsp oil
2 tbsps curry powder, or to taste
2 chicken stock cubes
600ml/1 pint hot water
Pinch of salt
4 tsps Weight Watchers from Heinz Thin
    Cut Orange Reduced Sugar Marmalade

1. Cook the onions and garlic gently in
the oil until beginning to soften.

2. Stir in the curry powder and continue
cooking, stirring well, for 3-4 minutes.

3. Dissolve the stock cubes in the hot
water and pour into the onion mixture.

4. Bring to the boil, lower heat and
simmer for 20 minutes or until well
reduced and thickened.

5. Season to taste and stir in Reduced
Sugar Marmalade.

6. Serve hot.

TIME: Preparation and cooking takes 30 minutes.

CALORIES: 52 per serving.

SERVING IDEA: Garnish with coriander and serve with grilled or steamed
fish or with hard-boiled eggs.

TOMATO SAUCE

*This weight watchers' sauce is a great standby and can
be used to enliven many different dishes.*

SERVES 4

1 onion, chopped
2 cloves garlic, crushed
1 tsp oil
1 x 295g can Weight Watchers from Heinz
Tomato Soup
1 bayleaf
Pinch of dried thyme or marjoram
2 tbsps lemon juice
1 tbsp chopped fresh herbs, e.g. basil,
parsley, chives etc.
Salt and freshly ground black pepper

1. Cook onion and garlic gently in the oil until softened.

2. Add the Tomato Soup and dried herbs, bring to the boil and simmer gently for 15 minutes, adding a little water if mixture becomes too thick.

3. Remove bayleaf, stir in lemon juice and chopped fresh herbs and season with salt and pepper.

4. Serve hot.

TIME: Preparation and cooking takes 25 minutes.

CALORIES: 34 per serving.

SERVING IDEA: Garnish with fresh basil and serve with pasta, fish or hard-boiled eggs.

APRICOT-ORANGE SAUCE

This fruity, low-calorie sauce marries beautifully with pork.

SERVES 4

240ml/8fl.oz orange juice
2 tsps cornflour
4 tsps Weight Watchers from Heinz
 Reduced Sugar Apricot Jam
¼ tsp mustard powder
Squeeze of lemon juice

1. Warm orange juice in a pan.

2. Blend cornflour with 2 tbsps water and stir into the juice.

3. Simmer for 3-4 minutes or until thickened, stirring constantly.

4. Remove from heat, and stir in the Reduced Sugar Apricot Jam, mustard powder and lemon juice.

5. Serve warm.

TIME: Preparation and cooking takes 10 minutes.

CALORIES: 38 per serving.

SERVING IDEA: Serve with pork, or use to baste ham steaks while grilling, spooning the remaining sauce over the steaks before serving, garnished with orange rind.

CHEESE AND PICKLE SCONES

*These savoury scones would be good
packed in the 'ploughman's' bag.*

MAKES 16

350g/12oz self-raising flour
½ tsp salt
50g/2oz butter
50g/2oz Cheddar cheese, grated
4 tbsps Heinz Ploughman's Tangy
   Sandwich Pickle
140ml/¼ pint milk

1. Sift flour and salt into a bowl.

2. Rub in butter and stir in cheese and pickle.

3. Add the milk and mix quickly with a knife.

4. Turn dough out on to a floured surface and lightly knead 3 or 4 times.

5. Roll out to about 2cm/3/4in thick.

6. Using a 5cm/2in fluted pastry cutter cut out 16 rounds, re-rolling trimmings if necessary.

7. Place the rounds on a lightly greased baking tray, quite close together but not touching.

8. Brush each round with a little extra milk to glaze, and cook at 220°C/425°F/ Gas Mark 7 for 10-12 minutes.

9. Place scones on a cooling tray, cover with a clean tea-towel, and leave to cool.

TIME: Preparation takes 10 minutes, cooking takes 10-12 minutes.

ICE CREAM WITH BLACKCURRANT SAUCE

*This is a quick, low-calorie way to enliven and add
vitamins to a scoop of ice cream.*

SERVES 6

6 tbsps Weight Watchers from Heinz
   Blackcurrant Reduced Sugar Jam
1 tbsp lemon juice
1 x 1l box Weight Watchers from Heinz
   Reduced Calorie Ice Cream
1 kiwi fruit, peeled and sliced
120g/4oz fresh strawberries, halved

1. In a small pan, warm the Blackcurrant
Reduced Sugar Jam and lemon juice, until
the jam is melted, mix well and sieve.

2. Allow to cool, and pour over individual
servings of Reduced Calorie Ice Cream,
allowing 140ml per serving.

3. Top with the fresh prepared fruit and
serve.

TIME: Preparation takes 15 minutes.

CALORIES: 146 per serving.

TANGY RICE PUDDING

*These moulds, designed for weight watchers,
have a delicate old-fashioned taste.*

SERVES 4

1 egg
2 extra egg yolks
1 can Weight Watchers from Heinz No
    Added Sugar Low Fat Rice Pudding
Rind of 1 orange, finely grated
½ tsp ground nutmeg
½ tsp ground cinnamon
½ tsp ground ginger
1 tsp Weight Watchers from Heinz
    Reduced Fat Spread

1. Lightly beat the eggs in a mixing bowl.

2. Add the rice pudding, orange rind, nutmeg, cinnamon and ginger.

3. Lightly grease 4 small ramekin dishes.

4. Pour the mixture into the ramekin dishes, and place them in an ovenproof dish with enough water to come half way up the sides of the dishes.

5. Cook in the oven at 180°C/350°F/Gas Mark 4 for 30-40 minutes until set.

6. Leave to cool and turn out on to individual plates to serve.

TIME: Preparation takes 5 minutes, cooking takes 30-40 minutes, cooling requires 30 minutes

CALORIES: 140 per serving.

KNICKERBOCKER GLORY

*This healthy weight watchers' version of the classic ice-cream
indulgence is quick to make and lovely to look at.*

SERVES 4

225g/8oz fresh fruits, strawberries,
   raspberries, kiwi, peach, grapes, etc,
   washed and sliced if necessary
4 tbsps Weight Watchers from Heinz
   Blackcurrant Reduced Sugar Jam
8 scoops Weight Watchers from Heinz
   Neapolitan Dairy Ice Cream
2 tbsps virtually fat free fromage frais
15g/½ oz carob chocolate, grated
15g/½ oz mixed chopped nuts, toasted

1. Divide fruit, Reduced Sugar Jam and
Neapolitan Dairy Ice Cream in layers
between 4 tall glasses.

2. Top with fromage frais.

3. Sprinkle carob chocolate and nuts over
the top of each glass and serve
immediately.

TIME: Preparation takes 5 minutes.

CALORIES: 265 per serving.

FRUITY RICE

*This creamy, colourful summer-time recipe for weight watchers
is extremely quick to make and full of fresh fruit vitamins.*

SERVES 4-6

1 can Weight Watchers from Heinz
    Rice Pudding
4 tbsps low-fat yogurt
1 tbsp Weight Watchers from Heinz
    Strawberry Reduced Sugar Jam
240g/8oz mixed fresh fruits, e.g.
    strawberries, raspberries, peaches,
    redcurrants, washed and sliced
    if necessary

1. Transfer the rice to a mixing bowl and stir in the yogurt and the Reduced Sugar Jam.

2. Lightly fold in most of the prepared fruit, and serve in individual dishes, decorated with the remaining fruit.

TIME: Preparation takes 5 minutes.

CALORIES: 110 per serving if divided between four, 70 per serving if divided between six.

BAKED SPONGE PUDDINGS

These make attractive, low-calorie, warm winter puddings.

SERVES 4

60g/2oz margarine or butter
60g/2oz caster sugar
1 egg
60g/2oz self-raising flour
1 tsp oil
4 tsps Weight Watchers from Heinz
    Strawberry Reduced Sugar Jam

1. Cream the fat with the caster sugar.

2. Sprinkle in a little flour, beat in the egg, and then gradually add the remaining flour.

3. Grease 4 non-stick individual baking tins with the oil and divide mixture between them.

4. Bake at 180°C/350°F/Gas Mark 4 for 15 minutes.

5. Allow to cool slightly, then remove from baking tins carefully, and place on individual plates.

6. Warm the Reduced Sugar Jam, spoon over the puddings, dividing equally between them, and serve.

TIME: Preparation and cooking takes about 30 minutes.

CALORIES: 303 per serving.

YOGURT WITH BLACKCURRANT SAUCE

This is a pretty, low-sugar, low-fat, summer's dessert.

SERVES 4

480ml/16fl.oz pure unsweetened
   orange juice
4 tsps arrowroot
8 tsps Weight Watchers from Heinz
   Blackcurrant Reduced Sugar Jam
Liquid artificial sweetener to
   taste (optional)
600ml/1 pint low-fat natural yogurt

1. Mix arrowroot with 2 tbsps orange juice.

2. Bring remaining juice to the boil and add the arrowroot, stirring well.

3. Return to the boil, still stirring, and simmer until mixture thickens.

4. Pour into a bowl to cool, then beat in the Blackcurrant Reduced Sugar Jam, and add sweetener to taste if desired.

5. Divide the yogurt between 4 dessert glasses and swirl ¼ of the sauce through each portion.

TIME: Preparation takes 30 minutes.

CALORIES: 173 per serving.

SPECIAL FRUIT SALAD

This makes a lovely summer treat, even for those on a diet.

SERVES 4

½ ripe honeydew melon
1 medium banana
1 tbsp lemon juice
150g/5oz strawberries
120g/4oz canned peach slices in fruit juice
   with 4 tbsps juice
4 tsps Weight Watchers from Heinz
   Strawberry Reduced Sugar Jam

---

1. Cut melon flesh into chunks.

2. Slice banana and toss is lemon juice.

3. Halve or slice strawberries, reserving 4 small berries for garnish.

4. Drain juice from peaches and reserve.

5. Place all the fruits in a bowl.

6. Mix the reserved peach juice with the Strawberry Reduced Sugar Jam, stir gently into the fruit salad, cover, and chill lightly.

7. Divide evenly between 4 dessert dishes and top each with a whole strawberry.

TIME: Preparation and chilling take 30 minutes.

CALORIES: 69 per serving.

ORANGE JELLY WHISK

This is a rather sophisticated adult jelly, low in calories and with a bitter marmalade bite.

SERVES 4

480ml/16fl.oz pure unsweetened
   orange juice
4 tsps unflavoured gelatine
10 tbsps natural yogurt
8 tsps Weight Watchers from Heinz
   Reduced Sugar Marmalade

---

1. Pour about ¼ of the orange juice into a cup and sprinkle the gelatine on top.

2. Stand cup in a pan of boiling water and stir until the gelatine is dissolved.

3. Pour into the remaining orange juice and stir quickly to distribute the gelatine.

4. Chill until syrupy and beginning to set.

5. Stir in the yogurt.

6. Whisk the jelly to a stiff froth, preferably with an electric mixer.

7. Divide the jelly between 4 dessert glasses, spooning in a layer of 2 tsps of the Reduced Sugar Marmalade half way up the glass.

8. Chill again until set.

TIME: Preparation and chilling takes 45 minutes to an hour.

CALORIES: 100 per serving.

SERVING IDEA: Decorate with a twist of orange peel.

RICE AND FRUIT CONDÉ

This is a colourful dessert, designed for those on a low-calorie diet.

SERVES 4

300g/10oz fresh raspberries, puréed or mashed

2 cans Weight Watchers from Heinz No Added Sugar, Low Fat Rice Pudding

240g/8oz skinned and stoned apricots, puréed or mashed

2 tbsps Weight Watchers from Heinz Reduced Sugar Jam (flavour of your choice)

Sprigs of redcurrants and/or mint to decorate

1. Divide the puréed raspberries between 4 tall dessert glasses.

2. Add a layer of Rice Pudding to each glass, using half the total quantity.

3. Next add a layer of puréed apricots.

4. Fill up with the remaining Rice Pudding.

5. Spoon ½ tbsp of Reduced Sugar Jam on the top and decorate with the redcurrants and/or mint.

TIME: Preparation takes 10 minutes.

CALORIES: 210 per serving.

COOK'S TIP: Thawed frozen raspberries and canned apricots in natural juice can be substituted for the fresh fruit.

APRICOT ICE CREAM DESSERT

This is another quick low-calorie ice cream topping.

SERVES 6

411g/15oz can apricot halves in fruit juice
4 tbsps Weight Watchers from Heinz
    Apricot Reduced Sugar Jam
Finely grated rind of 1 lemon
2 tsps finely chopped nuts
Mint sprigs to decorate (optional)

1. In a blender, purée the apricots with their juice.

2. Warm the Apricot Reduced Sugar Jam and sieve it into the purée. Stir well, and add the lemon rind.

3. Serve poured over each 140ml serving of Reduced Calorie Ice Cream, topped with a sprinkling of nuts, and mint if desired.

TIME: Preparation takes 10 minutes.

CALORIES: 134 per serving.

FRUITS OF THE FOREST CHEESECAKE

These are low-sugar, low-fat, mini baked cheesecakes.

SERVES 4

8 tsps Weight Watchers from Heinz Fruits
  of the Forest Reduced Sugar Jam
60g/2oz raspberries and blackcurrants
1 egg
1 tbsp caster sugar
Few drops vanilla essence
360g/12oz skimmed milk soft cheese

1. Beat egg and sugar together in a bowl until pale and thick.

2. Beat in vanilla essence and soft cheese.

3. Stir in the fruit.

4. Divide mixture between 4 individual dishes, stand them in a roasting tin containing enough hot water to come halfway up the sides.

5. Bake in the oven at 170°C/325°F/Gas Mark 3 for about 45 minutes until set and firm to the touch.

6. Leave to cool, then chill until required.

7. To serve, loosen edges of each cheesecake with a knife, turn out on to small plates, warm the Reduced Sugar Jam and pour over each one.

TIME: Preparation takes 10 minutes, baking takes 45 minutes, and a minimum of 30 minutes is required for chilling.

CALORIES: 120 per serving.

COOK'S TIP: Any soft fruit can be substituted for the raspberries and blackberries. Use frozen fruit if fresh is unavailable.

SERVING IDEA: Garnish with a sprig of mint or blackcurrant leaves.

INDIVIDUAL BLACKBERRY AND APPLE TRIFLES

These light, fruity trifles make the perfect summer dessert.

SERVES 4

2 egg yolks
25g/1oz caster sugar
4 tsps cornflour
Few drops vanilla essence
285ml/½ pint milk
4 trifle sponges
6 tbsps cassis or medium sherry
150g/6oz frozen blackberries, defrosted
2 x 128g cans or 163g jars Heinz
    Apple Sauce
115ml/4fl.oz double cream
15g/½ oz flaked almonds, toasted
½ red apple, sliced

1. To make the custard combine the egg yolks, sugar, cornflour and vanilla essence in a saucepan.

2. Gradually stir in the milk.

3. Gently heat the mixture just to the boil, stirring constantly.

4. Simmer for 3 minutes until thickened.

5. Remove from the heat and cover to prevent a skin from forming.

6. Break up the trifle sponges and divide evenly between 4 individual glasses or small bowls.

7. Spoon cassis or sherry over the sponge cake.

8. Top with blackberries and a layer of the Apple Sauce.

9. Pour the custard over the top of the fruit, and chill for 30 minutes.

10. Lightly whip the cream and spoon over the custard.

11. Decorate with almonds and fresh apple slices.

TIME: Preparation takes about an hour.

INDEX

* These recipes use Weight Watchers from Heinz products